THE DASHBOARD EFFECT

REVISED SECOND EDITION

THE DASHBOARD EFFECT

TRANSFORM YOUR COMPANY

Jon Thompson and Brick Thompson

Blue Margin Media™
Fort Collins, CO
www.BlueMargin.com

10 9 8 7 6 5 4 3 2
First edition published in 2018
Second revised edition published in 2019

ISBN: 978-0-578-48508-9
Printed in the United States of America

Dedication

*This book is dedicated to Mary Sue Thompson,
who taught us more through her beautiful life
than we could have ever imagined.*

Table of Contents

Introduction

First, a disclaimer.

We're not a "unicorn" tech company, we haven't *gone viral*, and we're not from Silicon Valley. We're from Colorado.

But we have experience—thirty-plus years of entrepreneurship and executive management. We've secured over $80 million in venture capital and private equity, created a five-hundred employee firm that optimized telecom costs for enterprise clients, went big (then crashed) in real estate, and worked for the world's largest hedge fund.

So, we've been around, and we've learned some lessons. And if you're wondering about our names, we're brothers, the oldest and youngest of four.

At the end of the real estate boom (in the late *aughts*), we realized we were hitting the third quarter of our business careers and our "real lives" had already begun (a long time ago). We felt a growing urgency to reassess our life's goals and how we could best reach them. Analyzing the pivotal points in our previous businesses, we discovered a troubling pattern. After starting a company and growing it for 3-5 years, the daily grind would set in, and we'd begin searching for a newer, more exciting venture, only to repeat the cycle. As a result, we became *serial entrepreneurs*, a dubious label at best. Sounds too much like *serial killer*, which is appropriate given what it can do to a business with otherwise good potential.

We also realized we no longer wanted our burn-at-both-ends lifestyle. No more high-risk *hockey sticks*. We wanted high-odds success.

Over the subsequent year, we studied the rise and fall of other companies. We interviewed successful executives and private-equity pundits, and we observed everyone in our sphere of influence who had achieved significant success. Eventually, the tipping point between businesses that thrive and those that merely subsist came into focus.

Here's what we discovered. Apart from the high-profile home runs, those who succeed in business invariably share two common traits. First, they work steadily on a no-nonsense value proposition for roughly eight years or more. Second, they know their numbers cold.

We were surprised to learn that the most successful people in our sphere didn't get there by creating new business categories, and they intentionally resisted bouncing from one flashy idea to the next. They were heads-down and singularly focused. Examples include a friend who built an executive-compensation consultancy. She struggled for years, then broke through to become a leader in her niche, charging north of $1,000 per hour for her top people. Another develops geospatial software for the pipeline industry. He stuck with it for 10 years, ultimately creating a thriving business with over 100 employees.

Neither has graced the cover of Forbes, but they have created significant organizations and incomes to match.

Equally important, the successful people we know obsess over performance metrics. They don't rely on intuition or their ability to respond to a crisis. We observed this trait in spades during a year-long engagement with Bridgewater Associates—the largest hedge fund on the planet. Bridgewater achieved unprecedented success by operationalizing a philosophy they call "radical transparency," championed by its founder, Ray Dalio. At Bridgewater, every activity or process that impacts progress is measured and assessed, enabling the company to overcome issues methodically and efficiently. Though Dalio has been criticized as fanatical in his adherence to transparency, his results speak for themselves.

We're now convinced that success in businesses comes down to maintaining focus. We're further convinced that maintaining focus is best achieved by keeping performance metrics current and in plain sight. This belief became our guiding principle and the thesis of this book.

With our newfound perspective, despite our tech-startup DNA, we decided to launch our most conventional company to-date. Blue Margin, Inc. is a consulting firm based on hard work and high-quality output. We're not exponentially scalable and we're not dependent on inventing new technologies. Nor are we looking for the brass-ring exit. This time it's about working smarter. Sure, professional-services sounds a bit safe, and it's not what most venture capitalists covet, but we wanted solid, predictable success.

What we got changed our lives.

A Radical New Approach

History confirms that inventing the next big thing is a low-odds endeavor. Silicon Valley, though an epicenter of entrepreneurship, is strewn with the wreckage of countless failed startups, a fact most of us overlook as we're dazzled by headlines of the latest self-made, thirty-something billionaire. Ninety percent of venture start-ups fail, and many of the survivors limp along like the walking dead.[1] If that gamble appeals to you, consider playing the lottery. Having walked that road a few times, we'd rather leave those Hail Marys to the likes of Steve Jobs and Elon Musk.

Successful execution is what matters most, and it's what makes running a business compelling. Playing the game at the highest level is the biggest thrill, even if the game has been around for decades. Airbnb wasn't the first online market for person-to-person home rentals, but its execution was unprecedented. Excite, Yahoo, and Ask Jeeves came first, but none delivered as successfully as Google. Good, solid business ideas are everywhere. Good, solid execution is rare.

And more than any other tactic we've tried, good execution comes down to keeping score.

Great thinkers like Peter Drucker, author of *The Effective Executive*, and Charles Coonradt, author of *The Game of Work*, have long recognized this simple truth about business. That is, the more you measure, the better you perform.

Ironically, most companies treat their data like background noise. In fact, most business data (more than ninety percent) is left unused.[2] However, when you put your data to work and begin viewing your business through dashboards (not just at the executive level but at every level), something amazing happens.

We've experienced this phenomenon first-hand, and once we discovered the power of our data, we set aside conventional management techniques that had frustrated us for decades. Like Ray Dalio, we became fanatical about making our performance metrics visible—to everyone.

What would happen if you threw open the doors of your proverbial boardroom? What if everyone in your business was the *best-informed* person in the business? Could the way you keep score change the game? Could you take a common business and make it uncommonly successful?

Call it a business model, a philosophy, or at lot of hard-won lessons. We call it **The Dashboard Effect.**

We're now ardent believers that companies can utterly transform themselves by simply improving visibility into key metrics. In other words, in our experience, objective, data-driven feedback is the most effective means of improving motivation, decision-making, and a sense of ownership.

A New Vision

As recovering dot-commers, we now find our excitement through successful execution, rather than perpetually scanning the horizon for new opportunities. Having discovered that the business model is secondary to how well that model is executed, we're no longer compelled to jump off at every station in search of something new. Instead, the exhilaration that comes from taking off the blinders, not just for ourselves but for our employees (and our clients), gives us our thrill and our purpose.

The result is that we're now more passionate about our business than when we started several years ago—the opposite of our historical trend. We're exceeding our business goals, which has led us to redefine our *ultimate* goals. We're no longer focused on the exit. Instead we're building something that not only creates wealth, but empowers everyone in the business to take ownership of moving the business forward.

More importantly, through the power of The Dashboard Effect, we're finally building something we're truly passionate about, and we're excited to share that passion with you.

What You Can Expect to Learn from this Book

1) Why leveraging data is increasingly a differentiator among leading companies.

2) Why you can no longer tolerate "silos" in your business if you want to succeed.

3) How a culture of visibility can ignite employees' sense of ownership without the need for process-reengineering, micromanagement, or negative pressure.

4) How emerging technologies have made The Dashboard Effect more accessible than ever before.

5) The difference between high-impact dashboards *that get adopted*, and those that get lost in the noise.

6) How visibility can transform your company (and your life) for greater wealth and happiness.

SECTION ONE

The Dashboard Effect— Business on Steroids

Chapter 1

Sixty Thousand Screaming Fans Can't Be Wrong

"No! Not possible! Replay that!" So went the chorus from sixty thousand spectators in attendance, fifteen million viewers at home, and eventually the rest of the world. Odell Beckham Jr. had just made one of the greatest catches in football history. A forty-three yard, one-handed, fully-stretched-out-as-he-sailed-over-the-goal-line catch. Defensive interference flags flew as he secured the ball to his chest and touched down in the end-zone. Watch it as many times as you like, it still looks impossible.

Like all the great moments in sports (e.g., Michael Jordan's "The Shot," Willie Mays' "The Catch," Franco Harris' "Immaculate Reception"), Odell's catch was an illustration of what inspires the highest level of achievement not only on the field, but in business and in life.

Have you ever wondered why we spend so much time and money on sports? Why do we willingly endure grueling logistics and high ticket prices for the privilege of crowding into stadiums to watch *other* people play? We do it because of *that* catch, that moment when we see performance at its peak. And we don't have to wait for a once-in-a-lifetime fluke. Watch the NFL highlights and you'll see amazing heroics every week. Heck, *every game*! But why do athletics inspire the pinnacle of achievement? Is it the high salaries? If that were true, the Olympics would be a flop. How about the desire to win? Possibly, but we all want to win both in business and in life—it's our everyday obsession.

The reason we see greatness in sports is that the goal is *so singular and so concrete.* Odell Beckham Jr. knew one thing with absolute certainty when he made that catch—his team's score needed to exceed the opponent's before the sixty-minute clock ran out.

That's it. Two scores and a timer. Three numbers that drive a multi-billion-dollar industry. Three numbers that are up in lights, accurate to the second, and larger than life for everyone to see. Take away the scoreboard, play just for the fun of it, remove the end zones and the goal posts, and the whole thing falls apart. Sure, it feels great to throw a perfect pass (so we imagine) or to recover a fumble. It must be supremely satisfying to beat the left tackle and sack the quarterback. But take away the score and the clock, and no one will show up, let alone pay for parking and admission.

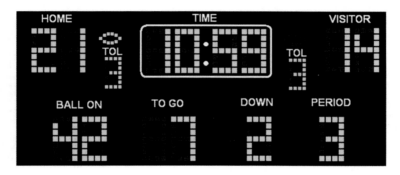

Figure 1. Scoreboards—the driving force behind great performance.
Source: Wikipedia Fair Use Image.

The same is true for golf. Nothing is more satisfying than driving a ball straight down the fairway (imagining again), but take away the greens and the cups, and it loses its appeal. You'll find something else to do, something with a goal. The same could be said for any sport, or for grades in school, or for trades on the floor . . . or for the annual review at work (wait, cue record scratch).

If it's true of human nature that scoreboards inspire peak performance, why aren't they used more at work? In the office setting, we inexplicably assume that what drives people to transcend limitations on the playing field no longer applies.

Instead, we emphasize job descriptions and compensation packages. We motivate with micromanagement and annual reviews. We do this because we rightly assume most people instinctively want to be productive and make a contribution. We wrongly assume, however, that the best way to capitalize on that instinct is to provide clear expectations and competitive salaries.

In fact, a study of fifteen thousand employees found less than a two-percent correlation between compensation and job satisfaction.[3] And it goes without saying that a dissatisfied employee is an unproductive employee. Accordingly, many prominent companies are increasingly dumping the annual review, deeming it counterproductive.[4]

Without some kind of scoreboard, employees won't achieve their full potential. Not by a long shot.

Chapter 2

The Secret to Employee (and Executive) Productivity

In his groundbreaking book *The Game of Work*, Charles Coonradt explores the impact of scoreboards on employee performance. Using real-world case studies, he illustrates how empirical feedback influences employee motivation and productivity. In his words, "If you want to improve the quality of performance in any area, improve or increase the frequency of the feedback."[5] Similarly, business-management guru Peter Drucker has long been credited with the adage, "What gets measured gets managed."

> "If you want to improve the quality of performance in any area, improve or increase the frequency of the feedback."
> —Charles Coonradt, *The Game of Work*

The benefits of being data-driven in business are well established. However, few companies succeed in harnessing their data to any significant degree. Why? Because keeping score doesn't happen naturally. It goes against our tendency to prioritize the urgent over the important. Shifting away from reactionary management requires change, and organizational change is an elusive endeavor. It won't happen without commitment and a proven process.

The science of transforming organizations by exposing performance data has been the singular focus of our company for seven-plus years, and the goal of this book is to share what we've learned so you can put your data to work, producing better outcomes while avoiding the mistakes we've made.

The Game of Work

Charles Coonradt originally founded the Game of Work organization in 1973 to address falling worker productivity in the Unites States. He discovered a key reason US workers were less productive than their foreign counterparts was their jobs didn't remotely mirror the competitive world they pursued outside work. Coonradt hypothesized that people naturally want to succeed, and that scoreboards lend concreteness to the otherwise abstract goal of "winning."

As Coonradt states, "There is something inherent in us to want to do things better, faster, higher, shorter, longer—and to win."[6] Empowering employees to achieve more isn't just good for business, it satisfies a basic human need. As Vince Lombardi put it, "If winning isn't everything, why do they keep score?"

Coonradt goes on to say, "It is a fact that those who keep score, whether they are winning or losing, win more over the long run."[7] Keeping score in business is simply allowing human nature to work in your favor.

One of Coonradt's case studies describes the predicament of a package-express company required to process freight bills as a matter of regulatory compliance. The responsible department struggled to keep up with their workload and perpetually lagged behind.

Coonradt's team was hired, and as their first order of business, they initiated performance tracking. Despite the manager's strong objections ("My people already work as hard as they can; requiring them to track performance will only add to their workload!"), Coonradt convinced the department to simply weigh the paper they processed.[8] He then defined a metric—ounces per person-hour—to drive the desired behavior. He plotted production on a graph, added a goal line, and displayed it prominently. Within two weeks, the department increased its productivity from a baseline of twenty-two ounces per person-hour to thirty-three. By week four it reached fifty-four ounces, and at the end of the engagement, the team exceeded seventy ounces per person-hour, an increase of over 300 percent, all without the use of threats, incentives, or process re-engineering. They simply kept score.

Just as keeping score can tap vast reservoirs of productivity, the opposite

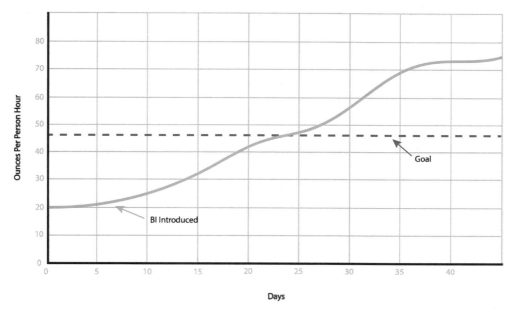

Increasing Productivity with Business Intelligence

Figure 2. Coonradt's Package Express Study from The Game of Work
by Charles Coonradt and Lee Nelson, 2012, Layton Gibbs Smith.

is also true. As Coonradt puts it, "People like playing games because they know the rules and the score…When we don't know the score, we tend not to want to play, or we play safe."[9] Businesses often fall victim to this trap. Executives and managers who understand the value of their data may assume that value only pertains to them. In so doing, they inadvertently forfeit the transformative impact of shared visibility into performance metrics across the organization, or what we call The Dashboard Effect.

A 2015 study of companies in the US and UK found that only 10 percent of employees are aware of their companies' progress in real time, and more than 75 percent of employees don't trust bosses who fail to share company data.[10]

Failing to share performance data is analogous to allowing only the quarterback to see the scoreboard. You can imagine the dysfunctional huddle that would result:

"OK guys, it's second down. We have one timeout, but we should save that for after the two-minute warning, which is 48 seconds from now. We're losing by three points, so we'll need a field goal to tie it up. Now get out there and do your best, and I'll update you before the next play."

Silly? Yes. Inefficient? Without a doubt. Wholly unlike business as usual? Surprisingly not.

How much better to share the scoreboard with *everyone*, drawing on the insights and initiative of each player and joining together toward a shared, measurable goal? That's what employees want, and that's how companies can better engage their most valuable resource. It's a simple tactic that's often overlooked.

The same study found that when employees do receive performance data, the frequency is low, and the medium is suboptimal. Only 15 percent see performance data daily, and less than 10 percent do so via dashboards. Yet over 50 percent of employees feel that sharing company information has a significant positive impact on their contribution, and more than 90 percent say they would rather hear bad company news than be left in the dark.[11]

Despite employees' desire for more visibility, many executives are hesitant. Convention holds that only those in leadership should shape strategy, that the job of management is to make sure employees perform specific functions, like cogs in a machine. Hence the elevation of the job description as a management tool. This utilitarian approach may be suited to focused, repetitive work, or high-risk situations like combat, but in business, where innovation and initiative win the day, it falls short.

What if you could pass the ball to your employees and free them to perform Beckham-like wonders?

What if you could harness the full potential of each person in your business? What if your company's brain-trust wasn't limited to just those at the top, but instead drew on the abilities of everyone, right down to the intern

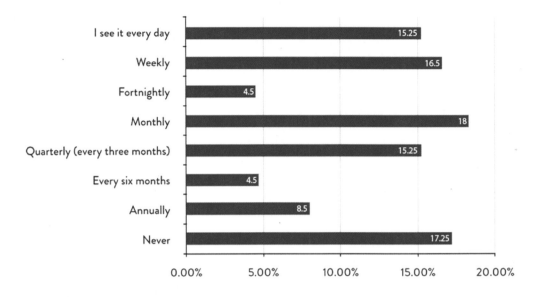

How regularly do you see performance data?

Figure 3. Sharing performance data with employees. (n=2000) (Whittick 2015).

sitting at his hallway desk? What if you could pass the ball to your employees and free them to perform Beckham-like wonders?

Transparency is quickly becoming the new standard in business and no longer the exclusive domain of vanguard companies like Spiceworks (according to *Forbes*, "The world's most transparent company," and according to *Glassdoor*, "One of the world's best companies to work for") and Zappos, the Internet shoe-selling phenomenon at the cutting edge of corporate transparency.[12] [13] These companies aren't simply bucking convention. They recognize that changes in society, corporate culture, and business technology make transparency a nonnegotiable when it comes to holding onto good employees and outperforming the competition. In the words of Scott Abel, Spiceworks' cofounder, "Being open and transparent is one of the best ways to build trust and engagement."[14]

The Bureau of Labor and Statistics states that the average job tenure for wage and salary workers is just 4.2 years.[15] In other words, the "gold watch" retirement is a thing of the past. As a result, employees are increasingly interested in benefits that go beyond salary and retirement. An *Inc. Magazine* study found that employees desire a sense of pride more than a raise. They seek coaching rather than micromanagement, and

> Companies that hold to an "us and them" culture will see employees moving on (statistically, every 4.2 years).

they want an opportunity for accomplishment.[16] Today's employees want a greater sense of ownership. They're taking ownership of their careers, and they're staking a claim alongside executives in making an impact. They increasingly judge employers by how much they value individual contribution and worker autonomy, and they consider themselves engaged in an equal exchange of value with those at the top. As a result, companies that hold to an "us and them" culture will see employees moving on (statistically, every 4.2 years).

Fortunately, breaking down the proverbial boardroom doors and inviting employees in is surprisingly simple. Start by setting aside team-building activities, org-chart flattening, and complex reward systems. Instead, elevate employees to a status that meets one of their fundamental needs by simply exposing performance data. Sharing the company's vitals establishes the equality and engagement employees seek.

This revelation will be a source of relief for anyone who has been tasked with developing and maintaining complex systems designed to incentivize performance. Through years of leading organizations, we've worn those shoes thin.

In one instance we created an incentive program around the rules of baseball. It provided a layer of abstraction we thought would transform oppressive sales quotas into an engaging game of base-hits and home-runs. We were convinced employees would enjoy the "game" so much they'd hardly know they were working! At the end of the first "inning" (i.e., the monthly sales meeting), as we called employees up to receive their checks and other prizes, it became apparent we'd missed the mark. Each "Congratulations! You scored a double!" or "Way to go, a home run!" was met with, "I did?" and "How did I do that?". Weeks of planning and organization. Zero impact.

The best solutions are often the simplest. A recent *Harvard Business Review* article addressed the often-elusive science of motivating employees, arguing against following convention in favor of leveraging data: "The solution is surprisingly simple: If you want to motivate employees, stop following your instincts and adopt a data-driven approach."[17] Still, for those who consider the chasm between executives and employees an unavoidable reality of corporate culture, embracing transparency may require a leap of faith.

This may help you take that leap. Transparency will not only meet your employees' needs, it will benefit your company tremendously. In addition to engaging employees and acknowledging their value, transparency will harness their fuller potential. In our observation, everyone has some brand of genius they can bring to the table, whether in leadership, interpersonal skills, positive energy, or good old cerebral horsepower. Invite them into the strategic discussion—pay them the respect of sharing the metrics on which the company's success depends—and you'll awaken an army of business "athletes." People tend to rise to expectations—making employees part of your "inner circle" does more to inspire initiative, hard work, accountability, and an ownership mentality than any other tactic we've tried in our decades in business.

> In our observation, everyone has some brand of genius they can bring to the table, whether in leadership, interpersonal skills, positive energy, or good old cerebral horsepower. Invite them into the strategic discussion—pay them the respect of sharing the metrics on which the company's success depends—and you'll awaken an army of business "athletes."

Coonradt demonstrated that dashboards not only bring focus to critical issues; they motivate employees in the same way scoreboards energize athletes and fans. That is, in addition to informing strategy, a good dashboard is the very vehicle that changes the behavior needed to execute on that strategy. This virtuous cycle is what we mean by The Dashboard Effect.

The good news, and what we hope to establish, is that getting on the data train is easier than you might think. As a friend of ours likes to say, "In business, you don't need to be a trendsetter, but you at least need to be trendy," and data is trending! The highest-growth companies we encounter invariably know their numbers, and they share those numbers liberally throughout their organizations.

Q: How can we be motivating our client's sales teams through showing report data?

Chapter 3

Moneyball for Business

Although limiting the exposure of performance data to just those in leadership will lessen the transformative impact of The Dashboard Effect, executive dashboards are a good place to start. Done right, they'll reduce reactive, bias-driven management among those who have the greatest individual impact on an organization.

As depicted in the book *Moneyball*, Billy Beane, the Oakland A's general manager who in 2002 famously used data to engineer an unprecedented win streak in the MLB, discovered that data and intuition often tell different stories. Rather than looking at the subjective characteristics valued by more experienced managers, such as body-type, "baseball form," or All Star status, Beane looked for characteristics that statistically had the strongest correlation to base-hits and wins.

Beane's genius was to let go of deeply ingrained assumptions in favor of empirical truths. He demonstrated that data analysis produces more accurate insights than experience and intuition alone.

We're all looking for a way to "hack" our worlds, to find a shortcut—the quickest route to the best results. In business, that process often takes the form of trial and error. We start with a hypothesis about how to increase sales or decrease customer churn, and if the idea feels right or aligns with recent experience, we put it into action.

Some initiatives stick, and others don't. We naturally drop those that don't *seem* to be effective and retain those that *appear* to be working. The hope is that our experience will produce better strategies over time, however incrementally.

If a debate arises over the merits of an initiative, arguments will often be subjective. One side might assert the current lead-generation program isn't producing *enough* leads. Another

> Without context your strategies are apt to evolve based on the most recent significant data point.

might contend that the program just needs *more* time. The problem is that "enough" and "more" are relative. How much better would it be to ask, "Is the new initiative producing better results per sales rep than during the same period last year?" or "Are sales trending toward defined goals at the expected rate?".

Without context, your strategies are apt to evolve based on the most recent data point (e.g., "I just pitched our new promo, and it's a dud."). Obviously one data point, no matter how painful, is not statistically significant, though our intuition might insist otherwise.

The problem is in how we process information. Our mental patterns can trip us up in countless ways. By default, we interpret information through our biases, which may suffice at an interpersonal level, but can wreak havoc in an organization. Psychologists have studied and codified dozens of common biases that shape our decisions.[18] See if you can identify with any of these:

- **First-impression bias**. People tend to attribute baseless significance to the first information they receive. You can observe this phenomenon during price negotiations, where the first number proposed "anchors" the range of what is considered reasonable.
- **Group-think bias**. This refers to the tendency to vet our opinions through the opinions of others. This propensity is the reason why at Blue Margin we prefer to interview people individually when gathering business requirements. Otherwise the strongest opinion in the room (and usually the most negative) tends to prevail.
- **Justification bias**. When people make a decision, or prefer one

choice over another, they tend to filter for data that supports their choice. If you google "red wine and longevity," you'll find reams of arguments for the health benefits of red wine. Search for "red wine is bad for you," and you'll find the opposite.

- **Ostrich bias**. To state the obvious, humans tend to avoid pain. In fact, research shows that investors check their portfolios less during market downturns. Although our reasoning for avoiding bad news may be rational (e.g., fearing it may be demotivating), common wisdom holds that proactively addressing problems as early as possible is the surest way to minimize the impact.

- **Proximity bias**. Our internal analysis engines often spotlight emotionally-charged events such as losing a sale or getting chastised by a customer. The tendency to assume that the most recent and significant data point can predict outcomes is the root of superstition. Lives are lost every year when hikers fail to recognize that weather can go from sunny and warm to cold and wet in a matter of minutes. Observe any roulette table, and you'll see otherwise rational people analyzing previous results to predict the future. The same goes for how we perceive economic trends. Our intuition insists the current state is our permanent state, even though history shows that economies invariably cycle.

To avoid making costly, bias-driven decisions at Blue Margin, we have adopted a policy of measuring everything we do (and equally important, only doing those things worth measuring). We're committed to this approach as a result of wasting countless hours and dollars on initiatives that never left the launchpad or that dragged on far beyond their useful lives. As a result, new initiatives don't see the light of day unless they can be tracked on a dashboard. And if they're not worth tracking, by definition they're not worth doing.

In addition, once we determine an initiative is worth tracking, the process of adding it to a dashboard forces us to define how we'll measure its success (e.g., How many leads do we currently generate on a weekly basis? How many do we need to justify the cost of the proposed initiative? And in what time-frame do we need to reach that goal for an acceptable ROI?). This helps vet both the feasibility and measurable benefits of an initiative.

Once an initiative is "on the board" everyone can see how it's performing. It can't be easily crowded out by the chaos of daily operations. Our scoreboards (displayed on TVs throughout our office) drive our thinking, conversations, and focus throughout the day, every day. This heightened awareness is critical because if you're like us, despite best intentions, much of your workday is spent reacting to issues. Once you're in the firestorm, instead of stepping back and analyzing the best approach, you'll likely try to outwork problems as they arise and rely on your intuition to prioritize on the fly. The reasoning is that once the insanity ends, you'll be able to analyze and adjust your strategy. But in business, the insanity never ends.

Sure, many executives set aside time for monthly or quarterly planning. They'll write down goals and occasionally review them, but won't typically keep them front-and-center and updated throughout the day every day. Even a list of initiatives displayed prominently will soon get overlooked. It will fade into the background, static and abstract, disconnected from your moment-to-moment work.

But dashboards are different. Dashboards connect your high-level strategy to your real-time effort. They keep you in sync with the careful plans you made when you had time to analyze your business. Dashboards give executives the insight they need to "hack" their businesses. They expose the drivers *under the hood* and support faster, more accurate adjustments.

> Dashboards connect your high-level strategy to your real-time effort.

Chapter 4

Transparency—An Idea Whose Time Has Come

Peter Drucker, one of the leading business luminaries of the twentieth century, made a career of promoting transparency as a foundational ingredient for success. Even though Drucker's books perennially appear on executive reading lists, and despite the increasingly crowded bandwagon of executives paying lip-service to corporate transparency, keeping information close to the vest is instinctual for most of us. Clandestine business practices that have long inflicted devastating damage on employees and economies alike, as evidenced by the need for legislation such as the Sarbanes-Oxley Act, requiring companies to provide greater visibility into their performance numbers.

When executives resist openness, the results can be disastrous. Overcoming that resistance is the hallmark of today's most successful leaders. As exemplified by the "maker" movement, where anyone with enough gumption can overcome long-accepted limitations, shattering the status quo is increasingly a virtue. People are less tolerant of structures and systems previously considered nonnegotiable, and transparency is the preferred means for innovative business leaders to root out inefficiencies and sleuth the shortest path to success.

> The hackers of the business world are pulling back every veneer and getting their hands on the machinery underneath.

With easy access to tools that accelerate progress (e.g., 3-D printers, robotics, compute power, artificial intelligence, and "apps" for almost anything), we have the means to innovate at an unprecedented rate. As a result, the *hackers* of the business world are pulling back every veneer and getting their hands on the machinery underneath.

Improving business processes requires objective insight into what's working and what's not. Data is becoming the most accessible window to that insight. However, for most businesses, that window is still cloudy. This is due in part to the overwhelming volume of data companies generate. According to IBM, "ninety percent of the data that exists in the world today has been created in the last two years."[19]

Today's data flows automatically out of almost everything we do. This truly is the data age, and paper is no longer the medium for moving information. Shut down your Internet router for a few minutes and see how quickly people emerge disoriented from their offices and cubicles.

> This truly is the data age, and paper is no longer the medium for moving information.

Fortunately, the tools needed to corral data and put it to good use are rapidly becoming more practical. The business establishment, though sometimes slow to change, is starting to embrace these tools. Without needing a team of data gurus, and with minimal investment, companies now have the ability to quickly zero in on the metrics that most influence progress, and to make those metrics easily consumable to those who most affect outcomes. For the first time in history, virtually every business has the means to leverage the power of data analytics and dashboards.

The business intelligence industry is evolving quickly to the growing demand for better data tools. From do-it-yourself dashboards to open-source analytics, to plug-and-play machine learning and artificial intelligence, what used to be the exclusive domain of the largest companies is now accessible to even small and midsized companies.

Data's Perfect Storm

One reason for the growing proliferation of data-analysis tools is a massive shift toward Software as a Service (SaaS) or the "Cloud" (i.e., hosted software applications that replace complex software and servers with turnkey services). This shift is due in part to the growing proliferation of apps, the ubiquity of broadband, and the popularity of portable devices. Employees now use an average of 3.5 electronic devices to do their work, and free Wi-Fi at coffee shops and airports has morphed from luxury to inalienable right.[20] These changes have dramatically increased our access to data and have helped make SaaS the new norm. And SaaS data tools have made The Dashboard Effect exponentially more viable than was previously possible with on-premises computing.

Consider Slack, a team-based instant messaging software company. Slack has been one of the fastest-growing companies in the world, achieving a valuation of nearly $3.8 billion after its first twenty-nine months of operation.[21] The reason? Companies want employees to work more transparently, and services like Slack, delivered in the Cloud, ease that process.

Not surprisingly Slack's CEO, Stewart Butterfield, points to transparency as the key to business success: "[We] all need communication to be visible to everyone in the company, across all hierarchical levels, and across all departments."

However, messaging platforms alone won't provide enough visibility to create The Dashboard Effect. Some level of automation is needed to maintain transparency as your company scales, and dashboards are well-suited to this purpose. They bring key issues to the surface and put your company's performance metrics up in lights, replacing the need for countless messages and meetings to get everyone working from the same playbook. Well-designed dashboards align everyone's efforts, automatically.

> Well-designed dashboards align everyone's efforts, automatically.

As more companies understand the potential hidden in their data, the field of business intelligence will continue to evolve in response.

Consider the following statistics:

- Nearly eight in ten executives agree or strongly agree with the statement. *If we could harness all of our data, we would be a much stronger business.*[22]

- 67 percent of North American businesses are interested in using advanced analytics to improve business operations.[23]

It's little wonder *Harvard Business Review* recently labeled Data Scientist "the sexiest job of the twenty-first century." [24] Similarly, according to Glassdoor, the online employee-placement behemoth, Data Scientist ranked as the "best job of the year" for both 2016 and 2017.[25]

But We Already Have Reports Coming Out Our Ears!!!

If your company is like most, you own or subscribe to a plethora of applications to help run your business. Although we're all searching for the panacea—a single platform that does everything from accounting to sales to project management—that goal isn't realistic in most cases. Show us a company with an ERP system (Enterprise Resource Planning, or *the single piece of software that does everything*), and we'll show you a company that's still herding countless other software systems.

These systems produce a constant stream of data that overwhelms most companies. To help mitigate this burden, most software systems offer reporting modules, and in some cases, "business intelligence" modules. Almost every CRM system, for example, comes with a bevy of canned reports and graphs to help make sense of the data. The same goes for accounting software, point-of-sale systems, time tracking tools, web-traffic monitoring services, ad nauseam. However, most companies struggle to make good use of these reporting tools. Why? Because they aren't easy enough.

When getting your hands on the data requires too much overhead, jumping from one system to the next, exporting data and manipulating it in Excel, requesting reports from IT, or mentally calculating insights from rows and columns, you'll quickly fall off the data train. That's why bolt-on reporting tools scattered across countless systems often fail to get adopted. Simplicity is the missing ingredient.

In a reactive management mode (i.e., business as usual), despite innumerable tools for increasing productivity, people usually deal first with whatever is flapping around and making the most noise in front of them. Regardless of your *Seven Habits* habit, your *Franklin-Planner* planning, your *Getting Things Done* thing, or your latest "10 Best Apps to Boost Productivity," we all get overwhelmed sometimes, unless you're Ben Franklin (though seriously, how long did he *really* implement his new-habit-every-day plan?). Asking people to add to their daily burden is the first misstep that results in failed data initiatives.

> People usually deal first with whatever is flapping around and making the most noise in front of them.

SECTION TWO

Shifting to a Data-Driven Culture

Chapter 5

It Takes More than Words

Integrity. Communication. Respect. Excellence.

Recognize those words? Those four words were inscribed on the lobby wall at Enron.

After a decade tarnished by the demise of countless multinational corporations and an economic crash precipitated by unethical business practices, many high-profile companies are embracing the values of transparency. Companies like Twitter, Airbnb, and Google are known for taking transparency very seriously. They live by its tenets and charge their employees to be its ambassadors.

Transparency, like it or not, is trending. Twitter keeps politicians more accountable, Google reviews keep businesses more honest, and Facebook plays an endless loop of our "private" lives for all the world to see. Transparency is no longer a matter of choice, and once embraced, it can be your greatest asset.

> Developing a healthy, open culture is increasingly taking center stage in the quest to build successful companies.

There is a shift taking place in business, from secretive, top-down power structures to environments where trust and transparency are the stronger currencies. Developing a healthy, open culture is increasingly taking center stage in the quest to build successful companies. And emerging business intelligence tools are making that goal more viable than was previously possible.

Transparency—The Latest Disruption

Consider Buffer, a social media company that has adopted a level of transparency most people would consider borderline reckless. As part of their commitment to remaining transparent, Buffer displays a real-time feed of all business transactions on their public website, as well as a list of each employee's salary. According to Buffer's leadership, "Transparency is a core value we've chosen to have, and we strive to live by that value regardless of whether we are seeing growth or going through a difficult period."[26]

Cofounder Leo Widrich points to practical ways transparency has benefitted the company. "When we published all salaries online, I think in that month we had four thousand people wanting to work for Buffer. People were coming to us saying, 'I know more about your company than about the company that I'm working for right now.'"[27]

Buffer also openly publishes a detailed breakdown of where every dollar of revenue goes. They believe being transparent with the minutia gives customers the confidence to trust the bigger, overlying structure. That belief has been substantiated by Buffer's extraordinary success.

HubSpot, arguably the most successful content-marketing platform on the market, takes a similar approach. In the words of its founder, Dharmesh Shah:

> At HubSpot, we practice "extreme transparency," making almost every piece of information about the business available to every employee. It's an unorthodox approach, but one that's saved countless meetings, attracted better employees, and stopped us from making a few really terrible decisions.[28]

One of the greatest benefits of transparency is employee satisfaction. Author and human-resources analyst, Josh Bersin, in his article "Thrive: How to Build a Simply Irresistible Organization"

"Only 13 percent of employees worldwide are 'highly engaged' at work."
—*Gallup Research*

summarizes the importance of creating an organization where people enjoy their work. Bersin shows that doing so isn't simply an altruistic pursuit—it's good business. According to Bersin's research, "The '100 Best Places to Work' outperformed the S&P 500 over four-fold from 1990 to 2009." Bersin also notes that for 79 percent of businesses, employee engagement and retention is the number-two concern after leadership.[29] Despite this statistic, Gallup Research shows that only 13 percent of employees worldwide are "highly engaged" at work.[30]

Two of the five elements for a successful culture as described by Bersin point to the need for transparency.[31] They are meaningful work and leadership that can be trusted. Measurement creates meaning. Just as keeping score drives athletic competition, tracking performance in business makes progress tangible. Providing visibility into performance metrics gives employees concrete evidence that they're making an impact. Obscuring those metrics diminishes the meaning of work and increases uncertainty.

Similarly, transparency creates a tangible foothold for trust to grow. Millennial employees in particular seek the opportunity to participate in programs that break down walls and give them a voice. No amount of "funny hat days" or "happiness ambassadors" will deliver the cultural benefits that transparency brings. Companies are catching on, and business culture is becoming more amenable to sharing performance metrics with everyone.

Neil Patel of *Fast Company* puts it this way, "The reason why transparency is so appealing is largely due to cultural trends and human behavior. We like people who are transparent, so it makes sense that we like companies who are transparent, too. It's not about some new 'hack' or 'technique.' It's about being a real person, a real leader, and a real company." [32]

Despite the success of companies like Buffer and HubSpot, most businesses don't start from a baseline of transparency. One reason might be that transparency requires exposing the good *and* the bad, warts and all. Being transparent often goes against our instincts, and many companies are unwilling to be known to such a degree. But therein lies an opportunity for differentiation—the rewards that come from being transparent with your employees and customers can be tremendous.

Try posting a dashboard of your company's key performance metrics in your office common area. We bet you'll see greater focus and an increased sense of ownership from your team in a matter of days.

Changing Your Data Paradigm

Despite the recent surge in available business intelligence tools, according to *MIT Technology Review*, 95.5 percent of business data is never used, leaving a monumental opportunity untapped.[33] Those who harness that data can gain a competitive advantage.

Virtually every business has ready access to the tools needed to leverage their data. But capitalizing on that opportunity requires an awareness of those tools and a new mindset. First, a company needs to recognize the value of its data. Second, it needs to invest the time and

> Once in place, today's data tools are largely automated.

resources needed to stand up the systems that make data easy to organize and understand. Yes, it's difficult to take time away from working *in* your business to work *on* your business, but once in place, today's data tools are largely automated, pushing critical insights in real time to those who need them most.

The most progressive companies are embracing data transparency, and those who want to remain relevant are quickly following suit. According to James O'Toole, a professor at the Marshall School of Business, "What we know about organizations in general is that the more knowledge workers have, the more likely it is they [will] make better decisions and the more likely [they will] feel invested in the work."[34]

That said, following the latest trends doesn't necessarily deliver. Consider Buffer's and Zappos' infamous forays into *Holacracy*. They experienced suboptimal results that ended in a hasty retreat for Buffer and difficult times for Zappos.[35] Deconstruction for its own sake can edge toward anarchy, and the resulting *non-systems* tend to disappoint (still, kudos to those who are willing to explore new frontiers, especially when they're willing to share what they've learned, as both Zappos and Buffer have done).

However, on this side of the borderlands, companies are increasingly experimenting with the concept of *radical transparency* and reaping its rewards. Leading companies such as Bridgewater Associates, have meticulously codified and operationalized transparency, leveraging their data to take the lead in their industries (you can read more about Bridgewater's approach in the bestselling book *Principles: Life and Work,* by founder Ray Dalio).

Nonetheless, there's no magic wand with data. Organizing your data, distilling it to actionable dashboards, and making it accessible to others requires careful methodology. Fortunately, the average professional is no longer beholden to the IT department to make use of their data. Business intelligence has been removed from its "black box" and is quickly becoming accessible to anyone who needs it.

Chapter 6

Blue Margin—A Case Study in Transparency

Leveraging Transparency

Developing the discipline and systems to bring data to the forefront of your business is analogous to earning your instrument rating as a pilot. To do so, student pilots must learn to fly using the instrument panel rather than visual cues from outside the plane. When a pilot becomes disoriented, the urge to panic and revert to instinct can be overwhelming.

John Kennedy Jr.'s fatal crash on July 16, 1999, for example, was likely due to the lack of a visual horizon, causing him to become spatially disoriented.[36] When this happens, pilots can quickly regress. They'll ignore their instruments, convinced they must be wrong. To avoid such tragedies, pilots are trained to instead ignore their intuition—their outside-the-cockpit vision and their inner ear—and focus solely on their instruments. Instrument training takes time because it conflicts with habits and instinct.

When it comes to running a business, managers and executives with poor visibility, like novice pilots, can find themselves flying blind, relying on instinct instead of information.

According to the Small Business Association, "Half of all entrepreneurs fail in the first five years."[37] Ask any business veteran why and they'll likely cite *lack of execution* as the primary issue. Successful execution requires visibility. Successfully managing a business depends on being able to see what's working, what's not, and what needs to change. This is why private equity firms, after acquiring a company, start by requiring regular performance reports.

Through experience, they've learned that not knowing the numbers puts a company at risk.

The road to business success is littered with the ruins of good ideas that were poorly executed. How many epiphanies about the *next big thing* have you experienced in your life, only to see "your" idea succeed in the hands of someone who actually delivered (one of the authors of this book would be the world-famous inventor of the *endless lap pool* if his ideas had become action twenty-five years ago).

Although some level of business acumen and ambition is needed, successful execution largely comes down to maintaining an honest view of performance. Without visibility, fundamentals slip through the cracks in the pandemonium of operating a company. Without an in-your-face scoreboard highlighting where you're falling short and where you're seeing the most success, executives won't be able to make adjustments quickly enough to survive.

> Without visibility, fundamentals slip through the cracks in the pandemonium of operating a company.

Just as data helps executives and managers operate more effectively, exposing data to individual departments and employees can improve performance throughout an organization. But providing effective feedback requires intentionality and technique. Simply disseminating dashboards to every employee won't guarantee results. You'll also need a process to make sure those dashboards drive the right behavior and a mechanism to help employees convert insights into strategy and action. This requires some art and some science, both of which are described in the second half of this book.

A Cautious Experiment

When we started Blue Margin, we understood the principle that transparency produces better outcomes. However, *understanding* and *implementing* are two different animals. Creating a healthy, transparent culture takes intention, and defining that culture is the first step. Once defined it can be measured, and once measured it can be managed.

Early on, we discovered that dashboards might hold the power to transform our business. We were in our conference room, slicing and dicing our data to decide how best to navigate the business. We were asking the usual questions. What marketing campaigns should we focus on? Which service areas should we drop, and where should we invest further? What industries and companies defined our target-market?

Rather than relying on intuition alone, we dug into the data and let it speak to us. The process was energizing. We felt like we were cracking the code on our business.

Then it hit us. *Why not give our employees these same insights?* Maybe they'd be inspired too. Moments like these were the genesis of The Dashboard Effect. Despite our years of experience in business-as-usual, we were developing a growing suspicion that giving the keys to the kingdom (i.e., our data) to everyone in the business was the shortest path to success.

However, something told us these radical impulses were dangerous, so we fought against them, surprised by our lapse of judgement and obvious naïveté. Surely the only place to discuss the really important issues was behind closed doors—issues like our growing expenses, employee performance issues, and (*is the door shut?*) our faltering sales funnel. Why else would every manager we'd ever worked with do it that way?

Over time, we began questioning whether our conventional us-versus-them perspective was optimal. Was it really the best way to reach our goals? After all, we became entrepreneurs specifically to avoid landing in the *them* camp. So why create a company that put our employees there?

We wanted a company full of people as engaged as we were. We didn't want to micromanage anyone, and we specifically didn't want to wear ourselves thin trying to filter and spin the information coming out of our boardroom.

> We increasingly question any management strategy that shields information from employees.

We wanted a team of equals who were each part of our inner circle, and we knew that to avoid becoming slaves to our business, we needed more of *us*. So, little by little, fighting against our instincts for how business is "supposed to work," we invited our employees into the sanctum sanctorum of our business. The results have been astonishing, so much so that we increasingly question any management strategy that shields information from employees.

Out with the Old

So how did we get out of our boardroom mentality and create a more visible culture? We questioned traditional assumptions about how businesses should run, and we began identifying changes that would most profoundly impact performance.

First, we reexamined our assumptions about top-down management.

We rejected the long-established privileges of the executive ranks in favor of harnessing the full potential of our people. We discovered that an old-guard power structure is difficult to dismantle because those who must change (*ehem*, us) are firmly attached to its privileges. Traditionally, the higher the rank, the greater the freedom from scrutiny and accountability. But in our experience, less accountability meant lower performance, and we couldn't credibly hold our employees to a higher standard while hiding behind our titles.

Although it seemed risky to openly share our personal performance with our employees, we took comfort from the example set by Bridgewater Associates. There, whether you're Ray Dalio, the former US Assistant Attorney General (and future FBI Director; yes, he worked there), or a twenty-something hire fresh out of college, your personal performance dashboard (which includes something Bridgewater calls your "Baseball Card") is available for everyone else to see.

Then we began viewing our employees in a different light.

In one sense, we treat our employees like volunteers. Why? Because we understand they are here by choice. The job market is diverse and dynamic, and because we strive to only hire exceptional people, they have the option to take their talents elsewhere. Like it or not, employees are free agents. The most talented are not content to simply trade their time and abilities for salary and benefits. They expect more. They want meaningful work, a good culture, and a reason to bring their A-game daily. As owners, we want that too.

We decided to make our employees virtual partners, rather than captives beholden to a paycheck. We wanted them to be as committed to making the business successful as we are. We wanted to offer an equal exchange of value, with the belief that our employees are here because they want to be, not because they have to be.

> We wanted a business that functioned whether we were present or not.

One important benefit of treating employees as equals is that the burden of leadership gets shared. Otherwise, the weight of developing new strategies and maintaining focus rests solely on a small group of leaders. We wanted help with that effort, and we wanted a business that thrived whether or not we were present.

Next, we gave everyone a scorecard.

In addition to the essential business metrics, we began measuring the performance of every employee, a controversial strategy, depending on your perspective. We also allow everyone to see each other's scorecards, and we display them on the homepage of our company's intranet and on large monitors in our office common areas. At our morning stand-up meetings and throughout the day, our own reality show plays on a constant carousel in the center of the office. And all our names are up in lights.

Figure 4. Blue Margin common area with performance dashboard displayed.

Some might perceive individual scorekeeping as too pointed or akin to public shaming. That's a good caution. Measuring individual performance can be a subversive scheme for behavior modification. Or, it can be an *open hand*. Your motives will decide.

If you love comradery, trust, and collaboration in the workplace, you'll find it through the equal footing dashboards provide. You'll discover that dashboards communicate mutual respect and reduce collective anxiety. They place everyone in the same proverbial boat, rowing in the same direction. Rather than laboring under the vague expectation to always increase output, our employees can see in concrete terms what they're responsible for, and each person can see how he or she is doing up to the moment.

If, for example, we want employees to wear suspenders with a minimum thirty-seven pieces of *flair*, we track it on the company dashboard—no guess-work required (gratuitous *Office Space* reference notwithstanding).

Uncertainty creates anxiety, and dashboards overcome uncertainty. Trust can't thrive in ambiguity, and a lack of trust invariably creates unhealthy relationships. The Unknown triggers our instinct to horde and protect. In a company, it pits employees against one another as each tries to protect the borders of his or her domain, uncertain of where those borders even lie. Dashboards, if presented in a spirit of respect, fuel the competitive element that drives individual achievement while simultaneously forging a team out of individuals. Each teammate is squarely focused on what he or she needs to accomplish while keeping an eye on the collective scoreboard and coming to consensus on how best to advance the ball. By openly sharing our numbers, everyone competes, everyone cooperates, and we all win.

> Uncertainty creates anxiety, and dashboards overcome uncertainty.

Most importantly, we lead by example. We, the business owners, are on the scoreboard too. The concept is radical, but it creates a stronger team, and it addresses the reality that executives struggle to be accountable and maintain focus as much as any employee. We can get lost in e-mails or mired by high-urgency, low-priority issues with the best of them. By making ourselves as accountable to our employees as they are to us, we reduce (even eliminate) the us-versus-them dysfunction endemic to many companies. This tactic more than any other has transformed both our culture and our output for the better.

We also became semi-fanatical about measuring every initiative in our business. A basic premise of The Dashboard Effect is that everything *can* be measured (not that everything *should* be, because there's a cost to the measurement and reporting process). In fact, when any new initiative is proposed, one of the questions we ask is whether it can be reasonably measured. If it can't, we question its value and usually pass. This filters out initiatives not worth pursuing. Again, we're taking a cue from Bridgewater Associates, where even the catered lunches are measured and evaluated (and are, not surprisingly, superb).

Finally, we gave everyone access to nearly everything.

At Blue Margin, every employee has access to virtually all our business data (excluding some HR data for privacy reasons). We've leveraged data tools to invite everyone into the proverbial boardroom. We avoid information silos like the plague. Everyone has the access to the information they need to fully bring their abilities to bear.

Then we did the same for our clients.

When was the last time you looked for a new mechanic? Beyond proximity to your home, what was the most important element you looked for? According to Consumer Reports, your number-one criterion was trustworthiness.[38] When taking a car in for repairs, you put yourself at the mercy of the mechanic. Sure, if they insist your *headlight fluid* needs changing, you'll guess something is amiss (hopefully), but if you're told your timing belt needs changing, you'll have very little basis on which to validate the recommendation. And after the work is done, unless you hear a strange noise, there's no way to know if the work was performed well, or at all.

> Just as visibility creates trust within a company, it does the same with clients.

The same is true for virtually every professional service. When your attorney or CPA sends a bill, you have little choice but to trust they did the work for which they're charging. If something feels off, you'll likely look for a new provider. Your clients do the same when evaluating the products and services you provide.

Just as visibility builds trust within a company, it does the same with clients. Still, when we began embracing the principles of The Dashboard Effect, we wrestled with extending transparency beyond our office walls.

While we keep a detailed record of all billable work performed, we worried that sharing that level of granularity might cause clients to scrutinize and question every minute charged. We would spend half our time, we feared, explaining why each minute was necessary and worthy of payment.

But we were wrong. It turns out that exposing detailed billing data to clients, whether they scrutinize the data or not, creates trust. Knowing they have complete visibility, they don't worry about the validity of our work. And if there is ever a question, the details make it easy to get back in sync. In other words, our clients don't have to blindly trust our word or feel they're at our mercy because we have expertise they don't.

Below is an example of the timekeeping dashboard we provide to clients:

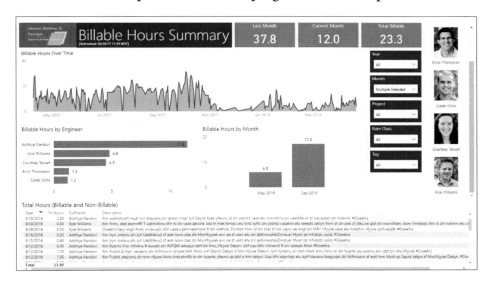

Figure 5. Sample client dashboard.

Compare the above example to receiving a bill for twenty hours of attorney services labelled "Contract research." To the latter, your reaction might be, "Really? *Exactly* twenty hours? What specifically did I receive in exchange?" You might feel compelled to call the attorney, complain, and negotiate the bill with minimal data to argue your side. And when that approach results in the invoice being reduced (as it often does), you'll be even less sure the original bill was justified.

As our fears around transparency continue to subside, we're bringing greater visibility into everything we do. In addition to sharing our billing details, we proactively call out our mistakes, even when a little spin could lessen the immediate damage. Here's what we've learned. Clients understand that mistakes happen. Rather than looking in vain for a service provider who doesn't make mistakes, they want to know how you'll respond when things do go wrong. Transparency is an opportunity to differentiate your company from the competition.

When it comes to acquiring and retaining clients, everything takes a back seat to trust. This principle is as true for banking, software development, and legal services as it is for car repair. And because technology makes transparency increasingly accessible, companies that don't participate are voluntarily limiting their ability to compete.

> Transparency is the fastest and most scalable path to lasting success, regardless of market conditions, the product or service you sell, or the maturity of your business.

Embracing transparency will require fighting the instinct to keep your problems under wraps. If you hold onto convention, the rationale for The Dashboard Effect may seem counterintuitive. It may feel like you're choosing the longer road when shortcuts are readily at hand. To the contrary, having observed and worked with hundreds of companies, we're firm believers that transparency is the fastest and most scalable path to lasting success, regardless of market conditions, the product or service you sell, or the maturity of your business.

Scoreboards at Blue Margin

Blue Margin is a professional services company, meaning our revenue is derived solely from billable hours. We have two basic goals for those hours—that each hour billed must deliver value, and that each hour that delivers value gets billed. Sounds simple, but it can become complicated, as any services company can attest.

How do you carefully track your time to make sure hours don't slip through the cracks unbilled? More importantly, how do you make sure you don't charge a client erroneously (a cardinal sin in our industry)? Also, how do you keep your staff busy and focused on the right activities? Conversely, how do you make sure you have enough staff to cover your contracted work?

If you manage a services company, you probably grapple with these questions daily.

To address these issues, we invested in a time tracking tool and audit each entry every month before sending out invoices. We found that time entries almost never overstate our work. Instead, our biggest risk was missed entries. Employees would sometimes skip making a time entry, planning to enter it later. After a day or two, those unrecorded details would become fuzzy or forgotten. With the sheer volume of entries and no way to easily codify them, we only took corrective action when something looked grossly awry. This reactive approach didn't address the root issues that kept us from tracking billable hours accurately and efficiently.

Our instinctive solution was to apply constant pressure on our employees to stay on top of their time entries. This was unpleasant for all parties, and it was far from foolproof. We constantly worried, with good reason, that the amount of free work we were delivering was putting our business at risk.

We needed a way to see, up to the day, if our time-entry process was on track and heading in the right direction. So, we developed a dashboard showing the performance of every employee (from the CEO down) and highlighted not just billable hours, but sales and marketing activities as well. We wanted to tell the story in pictures so that even someone from outside the company could spot issues at a glance.

We embedded the dashboard on the homepage of our company portal, made it the default tab for each employee's browser, and posted it on TVs around the office. This keeps our most important issue top-of-mind throughout the day.

We'll let you be the judge: can you tell how we did this month?

Yesterday Billable Hours	Current Month Billable Hours		
56	**1184**	Yesterday	**Month**

Billable Hours	[Last Refreshed - 10/26/2017 11:59 AM]			
	Billable KPI	Utilization	Goal	% Goal
Caleb Ochs	203.7 ⬤	93.4%	65%	143.7%
Adithya Nanduri	128.0 ⬤	95.3%	70%	136.2%
Lauren Dittmann	131.0 ⬤	94.2%	70%	134.6%
Courtney Tewalt	160.7 ⬤	85.1%	65%	130.9%
Kyle Williams	46.5 ⬤	25.6%	20%	127.9%
Paul Van Ryn	141.2 ⬤	77.5%	65%	119.2%
Sebastien Dutot	143.7 ⬤	77.3%	70%	110.4%
Josh Klenk	135.6 ⬤	76.1%	70%	108.6%
Landon Ochs	131.4 ⬤	75.0%	70%	107.1%
Kevin McManus	79.1 ⬤	100.0%	100%	100.0%
Brick Thompson	15.1 ⬤	7.0%	10%	70.2%
Grand Total	**1,345.5** ⬤	**66.6%**	**62%**	**107.3%**

Figure 6. Billable hours dashboard.

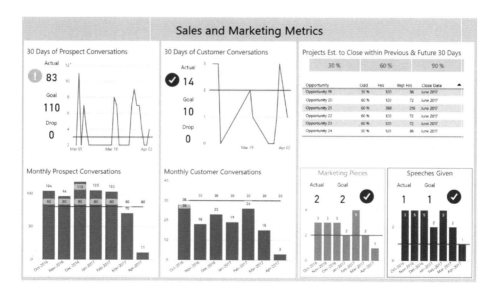

Figure 7. Blue Margin Inc. sales and marketing and billable hours dashboards.

Here's what we see: mostly greens and a couple yellows. From this snapshot, we can see we're doing well, but have at least one area of concern. We can see how each person is performing, and each person can see exactly how he or she fits into the bigger picture. The result is clear visibility into the company's vitals.

We no longer worry whether our engineers are logging their hours because they assume full responsibility for the success of their areas of the business. This results in higher job satisfaction because each person knows with certainty whether he or she is succeeding, and how to stay on track. We still audit entries to protect our clients, and we reward employees for mistake-free time entries.

> Real-time, self-administered accountability eliminates the need to pressure or micromanage anyone.

Real-time, self-administered accountability eliminates the need to pressure or micromanage anyone, which is a huge relief to our managers. Our people are happier because dashboards all but eliminated reactive management and all traces of boss-versus-employee sentiment in the office.

Bottom line, we discovered that employees are more effective and enjoy work more when they have the visibility needed to manage their area of the business. They prefer to be treated as grown-ups and will take on that mantle willingly, rather than subjugate themselves to micromanagement.

Most employees don't know whether they're truly meeting expectations. Worse, they learn to live with the looming presence of a manager who also doesn't know. For Blue Margin, The Dashboard Effect emerged as the most expedient means of eliminating those issues. Our scoreboards turned productivity into a sport. Now instead of battling the unknown, we're fighting for a common goal—green KPIs across the board.

Chapter 7

The Human Element

Despite the power of dashboards, we would caution any company against trying to automate the human element.

Mentorship is a hallmark of thriving organizations and it works hand-in-hand with dashboards. Good mentorship is the difference between merely aggregating the efforts of a group of individuals and harnessing the collective X-factor that propels some companies to uncommon success. And data provides a framework for healthy mentoring.

Simply adding *mentorship* to your list of company values will do little to affect change. Developing relationships that help individuals grow requires methodology. It needs to be operationalized or will remain an idea that never evolves into an enduring strategy.

At Blue Margin, we use several tactics to stay in sync with employees, and dashboards are the primary medium.

For instance, our teams start each day with a standing meeting next to a display of our most critical dashboards and discuss what's on deck. We're often surprised by the discoveries and collaborations that occur in these brief meetings. And our dashboards help bring clarity and focus to the conversation. The process strengthens the connection between us.

To bookend those meetings, at the end of the day, each employee summarizes in a few sentences what they worked on and how they are thinking about their work. These reports are automatically aggregated and broadcast via e-mail to all employees every morning. It gives us a view into each other's work. It also gives us a way to collect performance data not otherwise captured in our transactional systems.

The Accountability Review

In addition to our daily digest, every week each employee at Blue Margin meets with his or her manager for an "Accountability Review," or AR. The process is reciprocal, with the manager offering candid feedback to the employee, and vice versa.

The AR is a safe forum that fosters transparency supported by dashboards. Managers and employees agree upon goals and priorities, which are then added to each person's dashboard. From trial and error, we've learned that unless goals remain front and center (and up-to-date), they fade into the background, displaced by urgent issues that tend to assail us every day. Dashboards enable us to build on our progress up to the day, rather than just picking up where we left off a week earlier.

> Unless our goals remain front and center and up-to-date, they fade into the background, displaced by urgent issues that tend to assail us every day.

This process not only empowers employees, it reveals when an employee is a poor fit. Some discernment is needed to decide whether the AR is helping the employee make progress or simply exposing a mismatch of responsibilities. We're careful to withhold judgment and let the numbers speak for themselves. Without empirical measures, employees' mistakes can loom disproportionately in managers' minds. In fact, we've identified in ourselves a susceptibility to *flip the bit* on employees. That is, we can subconsciously view them solely through the lens of their most recent mistake, tainting our perception of almost everything else they do.

As managers and owners, we work hard to avoid this negative bias, because once the *bit* has been *flipped*, it's easy to lose sight of the whole person. In our experience, for transparency to have a positive impact, respect for the whole person is vital, no matter their shortcomings. Particularly dangerous is derogatory talk behind closed doors. Closed-door criticism is antithetical to The Dashboard Effect and should be cut off at the knees. Labeling someone based on a subset of their qualities obscures their fuller potential and is the foundation for prejudice. It also destroys the mentoring process. Dashboards help mitigate this tendency by providing empirical evidence of employees' contributions.

Lessons Learned

We've learned that simply deploying dashboards doesn't automatically create The Dashboard Effect. Certainly, providing visibility into performance is central to progress, and in a later chapter, we'll describe the tools for doing so. However, those tools won't help if your culture isn't in alignment. The art of visibility, the human element of operationalizing transparency, is where the rubber meets the road.

At Blue Margin, when we began extending transparency beyond dashboards and made it a centerpiece of our culture, our business transformed. Most significantly, our employees developed a stronger sense of accountability, the kind you expect from owners but rarely find elsewhere. Their ownership mentality brought an end to micromanagement at Blue Margin. To our embarrassment, we used to prefer that employees keep their office doors open to make sure they didn't wander down a *YouTube hole*. In retrospect, now that our employees have taken ownership of their work, we're amazed that idea once seemed reasonable.

Another benefit of increased visibility is that our employees enjoy their work more. As a direct result of The Dashboard Effect, our employees express that they feel as valuable as the owners and managers. Inviting them into our most important conversations not only validates their worth, it allows them to contribute in more meaningful ways. In our experience, treating people like

> As a direct result of The Dashboard Effect, our employees express that they feel on equal footing with the owners and managers.

cogs in a machine will quickly turn *employees* into *exployees.*

In other words, The Dashboard Effect doesn't just democratize data, it recognizes each employee as a whole person and leverages transparency to increase their engagement.

If turnover is trending upward and employee satisfaction is waning at your company, visibility is probably lacking. Dig deep and root out the problem. Institute transparency at every level. Commit to open discourse and measurable feedback, and you'll help employees take ownership of their work.

Blue Margin's experiment with transparency has convinced us of the overwhelming benefits of becoming data-driven and the need to never again drift back to management conventions that frustrated us for years. Through our experience, we've identified 5 characteristics of the data-driven business to make sure we stay on track:

1. **Measure everything.** If it's not worth measuring, it's probably not worth doing.

2. **Open the boardroom doors.** Provide transparency by exposing key metrics in real time, all the way to the bottom of the org chart.

3. **Treat employees like grown-ups**. Defining goals and tracking progress against those goals on a scoreboard is the surest way to inspire employees to perform at ever higher levels. Trust that each employee possesses some brand of genius and wants to put their talents to good use. Then give them the visibility they need to do so.

4. **Leverage technology to automate measurement and reporting wherever possible**. The most progressive companies are systematic about being data-driven. Be a pacesetter in your industry.

5. **Don't overlook the human element**. Automation is wonderful, but don't try to automate relationships. Commit to a simple, structured process for mentoring employees, and use empirical feedback to *touch the nerve* in ways that drive meaningful growth.

Figure 8. Blue Margin's Key's to Visibility.

Chapter 8

The Dangers of Non-Transparency

Cautionary Tales

We never cease to be amazed when clients insist on withholding performance data from their employees. We're even more surprised when we find that impulse in ourselves. It seems there's a latent distrust of transparency in most of us. In business as usual, distrust is a veritable institution, despite overwhelming evidence that a lack of transparency hurts progress.

Nonetheless, the most successful companies are overcoming their distrust of transparency. So why do we hesitate? Why would we willingly limit our success? Some may contend that the process of "managing the message" is intrinsic to effective leadership. The assumption is that given total visibility, employees will serve their own interests at the expense of the company.

In our years of observing executives (and ourselves), the status

> For many of us, the idea that more transparency (and more freedom) inspires a higher sense of responsibility is counterintuitive.

quo maintains that successful management is a matter of corralling perceptions and motivations; too much employee autonomy is by definition poor management. We assume that like horses, which when given free reign will wander back to the familiarity of the barn, most employees, given enough leeway, will seek their own comfort over the company's progress. For many of us, the idea that more transparency (and more freedom) inspires a higher sense of responsibility is counterintuitive.

However, what's true for horses isn't necessarily true for people. Sure, if you need to limit a person to a strict set of tasks, tight parameters may be necessary. But in most situations, imposing tight limits is a suboptimal way to draw out people's potential. For employees to bring their full abilities to bear, they need the latitude and the tools to think and act strategically. Rather than filtering data, we recommend exposing how the company is truly performing and trusting your people to respond like the adults they are (or *will be*, given the opportunity). The alternative is micromanagement and weak delegation, limiting the company's potential to those few who are *in the know*.

The tendency to adopt a closed-door culture is an outmoded management style that has deep roots in our collective business conscience. Most businesses we encounter operate this way. Intentionally or otherwise, they follow old-guard management practices, channeling information neatly within the confines of the org chart. Ironically, maintaining those systems is not only exhausting, it creates suspicion, politics, and other organizational pathologies.

Unfortunately, history is littered with the decaying corpses of non-transparent companies. To avoid repeating even a fraction of their mistakes, take a moment to revisit some of the colossal failures that have shaken the confidence of employees and the public over the past decades. Though familiar to the point of cliché, the following examples are worth reviewing for their common denominator. Each started as a bona fide business venture, but because transparency was not culturally ingrained, when pressures mounted, obfuscation offered an option too enticing to resist. The result was catastrophic failure, and worse.

Enron

Perhaps the most high-profile example of counter-transparency is Enron. In 2001, the Enron scandal shook the nation and the world and led to the complete dissolution of one of America's largest energy companies and several related enterprises. Initially, Enron saw significant success, thanks in large part to the business acumen of founder Kenneth Lay and the deregulation of the natural gas industry in the 1980s, which enabled Enron to sell energy commodities at unprecedented prices and profit margins. By 1992, Enron had become the largest supplier of natural gas in North America.

However, things were not as rosy as the numbers indicated. The drive for profits in the face of shifting market forces led to creative accounting that ultimately devolved into criminal activity. While it's easy to distance ourselves from the perverse thinking that led to Enron's destruction, most businesses grapple with ethical or legal gray areas at some point. Without a commitment to transparency, businesses may not navigate those waters successfully.

No evidence suggests that Enron was founded on false pretenses, and no single event or crossed-line doomed the company. Rather, it started with a lack of transparency followed by incremental decisions to hide the truth, ultimately resulting in disaster. Had Enron's management been more transparent with employees, auditors, and stakeholders when their market began faltering, it's far less likely they would have self-destructed so dramatically (or at all).

Lehman Brothers

There are few companies that illustrate the potential downside of opaque business practices as well as the collapse of financial giant Lehman Brothers in the opening days of the Great Recession. To those outside the company, Lehman Brothers was a resounding success—a small firm that built itself to towering heights with talent and hard work. However, beneath the polished exterior, a lack of transparency had taken root.

Lehman Brothers was founded by two German brothers, Henry and Emanuel Lehman, who immigrated to the United States in the mid-1800s. As a testament to the brothers' perseverance, the firm prospered into a global financial services firm, despite significant counter-forces including the bankruptcies of major railroads, two world wars, the Korean War, capital shortages, and the Russian debt default.

Lehman Brothers' growth came to a screeching halt in the mid-2000s

---

when the US housing bubble burst and the economy flatlined. Although external circumstances hurt the company, they were not the ultimate source of its collapse. The underlying problem came down to a lack of transparency that avoided much-needed accountability in the upper ranks.

The beginning of the end came in 2007. While the company basked in the glory of a $60 billion market capitalization, subprime borrowers were beginning to default. That trickle became a flood, and things went south quickly. Rather than accepting their circumstances and making changes to curb the meltdown, the company chose to manipulate shareholders' perceptions. At one point, the CFO told investors that the risk from the subprime market drawdown was contained and would have little, if any, impact on the company.

Despite raising billions from investors to increase liquidity, the company slid further. The first week of September 2008 saw the company's stock plunge by 77 percent, and its freefall continued after the Korea Development Bank put a halt to negotiations to buy a stake in the company.[39] By Monday, September 15, 2008, Lehman's stock was virtually worthless, and the company was gone.

In the end, the headlong rush toward maximizing profits at the expense of transparency was Lehman Brothers' undoing, leaving billions of dollars in debt and an unstable global investment market. Had executives been honest with themselves about the risks of subprime loans and come clean to shareholders when the situation degraded, they may have survived the economic downturn as they had so many previous trials.

MCI/WorldCom

Before acquiring MCI, WorldCom was the second largest long-distance carrier in the United States, back when long-distance service was a strong profit generator. However, the company is remembered for something far darker—the single largest bankruptcy action in the country up to that point, outpacing the dissolution of both Lehman Brothers and Enron.

WorldCom was founded in the early 1980s and grew rapidly. Thanks to significant financial clout, it purchased numerous other firms, including MCI, a merger valued at $37 billion, at that time the largest in US history.[40] But the telecommunications market was changing, a fact that WorldCom refused to embrace.

As problems mounted, CEO Barnard Ebbers and other members of WorldCom failed to inform investors. In the ultimate display of non-transparency, from 1999 to early 2002, Ebbers and three others created false financial reports to hide losses. When the deception was finally discovered, it came in the form of $3.8 billion in accounting fraud, only later surpassed by Bernie Madoff's scheme (which bilked investors of $64 billion). For WorldCom, blatant dishonesty was at the core of their undoing. Perhaps dishonesty was a preexisting character flaw of its leaders, but had WorldCom as a company embraced transparency, it would have been a less fertile environment for fraud to take hold.

What's the lesson from these cautionary tales? Each is an extreme example and may seem disconnected from most of us. However, evidence suggests that each started as an honest venture. By not being deliberate about transparency, lines became blurred and were ultimately crossed. For most, a strong moral compass will prevail, but we shouldn't overlook the inevitable temptation to incrementally obscure the facts. When facing a crisis, we're all tempted to filter the bad news. In the cases of MCI, Enron, and Lehman Brothers, fraud was merely the final step. Along the way, executives chose near-term damage control over long-term transparency, resulting in tremendous losses both personally and professionally.

> In the end, transparency is the simpler, more enduring path.

Arguably, had these companies remained transparent through their difficulties, they may have persevered. While running a non-transparent company does not necessarily lead to criminal activity, a lack of transparency can unwittingly take hold and morph a company into something sinister. In the end, transparency is the simpler, more enduring path.

How Non-Transparency Takes Hold

At Blue Margin, when we stopped controlling information and began sharing it freely, our employees became more engaged, and our success accelerated. In decades prior, we had proven the inverse also holds true. This chapter identifies some common manifestations of non-transparency to help you identify ways you may be limiting your company.

Drowning in a Sea of Spreadsheets

As business intelligence consultants, we see the negative impact of non-transparency on a regular basis. One client, intent on using data to manage his business, asked for our feedback on the reports he'd developed. After a sixty-minute tour of his spreadsheets, we had little more insight into his company's performance than when we started (and it became apparent he didn't either). He was committed to collecting data and using it to improve his business, yet his methodology failed to deliver the visibility he desperately needed.

In a non-transparent business, information has a habit of getting lost in the system. It ends up isolated in spreadsheets, e-mails, voicemails, and the minds of key players. Each of these becomes a silo, where information remains invisible to the rest of the company. As the company scales, critical metrics and insights can become lost in an ever-expanding data haystack.

Faceless Collaboration and Inefficient Communication

Companies can limit their transparency by holding onto inefficient modes of communication. Although still essential, phone calls and e-mails are suboptimal media for many business processes. Like Excel files trapped on individuals' computers, they create communication silos.

In particular, e-mail overload is a growing menace. Take a look at your inbox. It's a simple tool, but likely the biggest hindrance to your personal productivity. Most of us are in the habit of e-mailing reports and spreadsheets, turning our inboxes into massive flat-filing systems, a jumbled repository of our most critical business data. This fractures the company, hurting collaboration and the flow of information. Although e-mail has its place, the problem for most companies is a near total dependence on e-mail for managing information.

> Although e-mail has its place in business, the problem for most companies is a near total dependence on e-mail for managing information.

Dashboards counteract the downsides of email. They offer real-time, shared insights into the most important information.

Convoluted Data

In addition to e-mail overload, most companies are burdened by the proliferation of disconnected, data-generating software systems. One reason for this proliferation is that most technology ecosystems evolve organically. Pieces and parts are implemented over time in a reactionary mode to meet needs as they arise. As the business grows and changes, new systems are added, and to avoid to disruption, old systems are left in place. When systems evolve in this way, each as a separate initiative, the process of gathering and organizing data can seem impossible.

Generating reports in such an environment requires brute force. This "hand carry" process is costly and can result in faulty transcription, multiple versions of the truth, and delayed insight. Automated dashboards will help eliminate those issues.

Dysfunctional Project Management

Even with a plethora of software and business systems, many companies lack a good system for managing projects. Their ad-hoc project management doesn't easily distill into a clear picture, instead consisting of a loosely coordinated labyrinth of Gantt charts, Excel spreadsheets, e-mails, meeting notes, and static reports. Maintaining visibility into capacity-versus-demand, projected workload, and job costing can be an excruciating process.

Easy-to-digest dashboards are critical for effective project management,

---

and we find it's often precisely what project-driven companies lack the most. Without a dashboard, project management becomes reactive, and much of a project manager's time will be consumed searching for and organizing project data rather than improving processes and driving deliverables across the finish line.

Limited Accountability

Without good insight into performance data, employees and managers are apt to deflect blame when something goes wrong and take credit when it should be shared. This problem is a symptom of limited accountability. Rather than staying in sync with employees, managers may resort to applying a vague and constant pressure to spur performance. Poorly defined success criteria put employees on unsteady ground and reduce those in charge to micromanagement. The result is sporadic, reactive interactions as managers try to keep employees on track.

Employees will have little incentive to take initiative if they're fearful of increasing uncertainty and pressure. Unlike athletes, the "players" in a non-transparent business don't always know the score. Employees

> Employees who can't easily check the scoreboard to see if they're winning, tied, or losing can't judge the risks and benefits of taking on new responsibilities.

who can't easily check the scoreboard to see if they're winning, tied, or losing can't judge the risks and benefits of taking on new responsibilities. The old sales adage, "A confused mind always says no," holds as true for employees as it does for customers.

According to Gallup, of 2.2 million employees surveyed, half indicate they don't have a strong understanding of what's expected of them at work. Even more surprising, the managers of those employees are "equally unclear about what is expected of them."[41]

To address this issue, companies often turn to the tried-and-true *annual review*. Despite being a mainstay in corporate America, the annual review creates many negative, unintended consequences. When supervisors and their subordinates can wait to address uncomfortable issues until the annual review, those issue can fester and compound. Moreover, a once-a-year analysis of employees' performance does not provide enough guidance.

By way of analogy, consider how effective Alcoholics Anonymous would be if meetings were held annually instead of weekly. Similarly, how productive would you be if you organized your task list once per year? How current would you be on developments in your industry from reading one business article every twelve months? The annual review does little to create real, lasting change because its slow cadence doesn't provide enough reinforcement.

> The annual review does little to create real, lasting change because its slow cadence doesn't provide enough reinforcement.

Detailed job descriptions are another go-to management strategy. It's easy to confuse writing down goals with actually advancing those goals. How many times have you written down a plan for getting in shape, improving your mind, or overhauling a key business strategy, only to discover that plan months later, forgotten and unexecuted? We tend to assume that if a plan is good, we'll naturally incorporate it into our work and execute on it. In our experience, if you don't actively keep your goals and your progress against those goals current and in plain sight, you'll drift back to old patterns.

While defining an employee's responsibilities is helpful, job descriptions do little to influence employees throughout their daily work.

Frustrating Politics

Ask any corporate veteran what problems plague most companies, and office politics will surely make the list. Politics in both government and business are about gaining and keeping power. To gain power, the politician reasons that vulnerabilities must be hidden. In a non-transparent business, vulnerabilities are kept close to the vest to advance personal agendas. These subversive agendas derail organizations because they prioritize the interests of the individual over the group.

To keep the scourge of company politics from gaining ground, embrace transparency and remove conditions for seditious maneuvering. Just as sunlight is a good disinfectant, dashboards are a good means of eradicating office politics.

A Final Note on Non-Transparency

Holding onto conventional management tactics for convention's sake comes at a price. Without embracing transparency and exposing performance metrics, companies will quickly lose their way. They'll set goals then let them slip into obscurity. They'll start initiatives without a mechanism to ensure the flywheel keeps spinning. And in the chaos, they'll inadvertently let a lack of transparency take hold.

By elevating transparency, you'll not only minimize operational and cultural tripwires, you'll empower your employees and attract better talent. The modern job market is as fluid as it is diverse, and employees are increasingly discerning. They'll go where they can realize their greatest potential and where they can have their greatest impact. Given a company that operates opaquely and one that upholds transparency, the choice is clear. Generation X, Y, and Z graduates aren't clambering for jobs at old-school companies weighed down by rigid hierarchies and siloed information.

> "Transparency is not just a buzzword; it may be a necessity for business survival in the 21st Century."
> —Glassdoor

Glassdoor.com (where employees can submit anonymous reviews of employers) has a unique view of trends in the job market. In their "Top HR Statistics" publication, transparency and trust rate highest among employee priorities. "Moving toward organizational transparency helps foster an environment of trust. Transparency is not just a buzzword; it may be a necessity for business survival in the 21st Century."[42]

Your Visibility Status

Having considered the impact of non-transparency, it's time to look in the mirror. Take this brief assessment of your company:

Visibility Checklist:

☐ Employees have measurable goals and understand how they support the company's goals. *—pending*

☐ Employees have easy access to performance metrics and know how they're performing on a daily basis. *— pending*

☑ Employees have a structured and safe framework to regularly give and receive feedback. *—yes*

If you checked all three boxes, you can be confident that you're on the right track. If not, you have an opportunity to leverage transparency for better results.

The Dashboard Effect

SECTION THREE

●●●
●●●
●●●

Designing Dashboards that GET ADOPTED

Chapter 9

Identifying the Core Issues

Why Most Data Initiatives Fail

Most data initiatives fail to get adopted for the same reason iPhones are perennially popular, inspiring loyal customers to wait in long lines for the latest models. Although competitors offer similar functionality, their phones simply aren't as user-friendly, at least according to the *entire world's* consumer base (if you're an Android loyalist or a Blackberry holdout, don't shoot the messenger; Apple really does produce the highest selling smart-phone models in the world).[43] People like stuff that's easy; if data is too difficult to access, they'll take the path of least resistance and focus on whatever hits their inbox.

> If your BI isn't easy enough, users will fail to adopt, and adoption is *the key* to creating The Dashboard Effect.

In other words, if your BI isn't easy enough, users will fail to adopt, and adoption is *the key* to creating The Dashboard Effect. Even mediocre dashboards, if adopted, can transform a business, while the best dashboards, if users fail to adopt, can be a massive waste of resources and will have the added detriment of increasing resistance to future initiatives. The goal is to implement high-impact dashboards that people use. Yet statistically, less than half of data initiatives achieve their intended goal.[44]

In addition to being easy, for dashboards to get adopted, they need to be compelling. Think about your daily processes, such as time tracking, meeting prep, and proposal writing. They all take a measure of discipline, except one—managing your e-mail. Most of us have developed an attachment to our inboxes that borders on addiction. We check it constantly and compulsively, and feel a little let down when nothing new has arrived since our last *fix*. Why is e-mail the desk worker's crack? Because it's compelling. It's current, it's personal, and (usually) it's relevant to the very things we're trying to accomplish. Dashboards share those same traits.

Consider the last time you loaded the *world's greatest app* onto your phone. Maybe you found a better way to assign chores to your kids, track what you eat, or find local restaurant deals. At first, you may wonder how you ever lived without it. Your consumer endorphins flow as you revel in the awesomeness of your new, indispensable tool (or toy). You preach its virtues to others and insist they convert. Then, a few days later, you inexplicably stop using it. Why? Because it didn't fit into your normal "flow" in an easy and compelling way.

That's what happens with most dashboards.

Creating dashboards that are both easy and compelling requires careful discovery and design.

Designing High-Impact Dashboards

Making a dashboard simple and compelling enough for users to adopt starts with discovery. When faced with a problem, most of us follow a standard pattern for arriving at a solution: we ask questions, do some research, brainstorm possible solutions, take a poll among trusted advisors, then implement the solution that seems best. Though this approach provides some structure, it relies heavily on intuition. Intuition is our most readily accessible problem-solving tool, and by definition it *feels* right. Conversely, more objective, methodical problem-solving models can feel counterintuitive. However, in our experience the latter consistently produces better results. Fortunately, there are many well-established problem-solving methodologies that can keep you from being led astray by your instincts. Popular examples include Ishikawa, Six Sigma, Agile, Kaizen, and 5 Whys.

Root-Cause Analysis

One of the most effective models for solving problems centers on identifying root issues. This technique is called root-cause analysis, or RCA.[45] RCA is a systematic approach for identifying the most fundamental (but still actionable) issues that hinder a goal. In other words, it's a means of reducing problems to a few foundational issues rather than a multitude of proximate issues. When defining KPIs (key performance indicators) and designing dashboards, you might instinctively start by assessing the efficacy of your current reporting and identifying areas that need improvement. This approach may result in some positive changes, but it won't likely address foundational issues. Failing to identify foundational issues will result in dashboards that don't effectively *touch a nerve*. And if dashboards are not viscerally compelling, odds are they won't get adopted.

Moreover, failing to unearth root causes will leave dashboard designers with poor visibility into the full scope of the problem they're trying to solve. This can lead to unintended consequences, or *problutions* (i.e., solutions that cause more problems). Problutions often take the form of "feature monsters" (i.e. solutions that include extraneous functionality and/or multiple ways of accomplishing the same task), because unstructured dashboard design invariably results in mapping countless features to a swarm of *proximate* issues. This approach may scratch the itch to start fixing stuff, but it will produce a diluted and ineffective solution. A better approach is to design for a smaller, more influential set of *root* issues.

> Failing to unearth root causes will leave dashboard designers with poor visibility into the full scope of the problem they're trying to solve.

One of the best-known models for root-cause analysis is the 5 Whys. The 5 Whys is a technique used in the analysis phase of the Six Sigma methodology.[46] The process calls for asking a series of questions to get to root issues, and it avoids jumping to a design until the analysis is fully fleshed out.

Popular problem-solving models span a broad spectrum of philosophies and techniques. In our experience, the particulars of the model are less important than the value of actually using a model. In other words, the barrier to successful problem-solving is most often the lack of a methodology, leaving intuition in charge and outcomes unpredictable.

To create The Dashboard Effect, we strongly recommend implementing a credible problem-solving model and training your team to consistently use it.

Chapter 10

The BlueCore™ Discovery & Design Model

Blue Margin has developed a root-cause-analysis model called BlueCore for designing data warehouses and dashboards. Our approach is nothing new under the sun. It employs established RCA principles, and it works because it's simple.

Successfully applying BlueCore requires a balance of structure and flexibility. Following your gut alone will cause your goals to quickly fade into the mist as you glom onto design ideas. Make the structure too rigid, and you'll get bogged down trying to tie every loose end. Feel free to borrow what works and leave or modify the rest, but be intentional about establishing a model for solution design that can be duplicated throughout your organization. Through trial and error and by incorporating the most effective elements from other models, we've settled on an approach that consistently produces dashboards that get adopted.

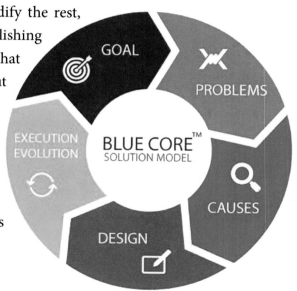

Figure 9. Blue Core Solution Model.

The Dashboard Effect

Tips for a Successful BlueCore Analysis:

Keep your eye on the prize. Throughout the process, remember the purpose of the BlueCore framework—to identify the simplest solution that efficiently advances your goals. In our experience, intuition-based solutions are almost always tragically flawed. They map too many features to too many issues, resulting in inefficient systems that don't get adopted. Using a framework that distills problems down to their fundamental moving parts leads to more durable solutions.

Keep it loose. This is a flexible framework, not a rigid formula. The trick is to stay centered on the business outcomes you're after. Defining your goals clearly and keeping them at the center of the process will produce the best results. Focus your thinking on the goals, and the rest will be simple:

1. Identify the problems hindering your goals.
2. Drill down until you get to *actionable* root causes underlying those problems.
3. Design your solution to address those root issues.

Feel free to "bend the rules." If someone jumps to a design, don't hit the buzzer. Just make a note of the idea, then carry on with the discovery process. If your root causes crisscross, overlap, or merge, don't worry about the mess it makes. Just keep drilling and the picture will come into focus. Also, remember to occasionally step back and make sure the overlying business goal is still front-and-center.

Avoid jumping to design. One of the snares of intuitive problem solving is "jumping to design." For whatever reason, intuition results in skipping to the solution before spending sufficient time understanding the problem. The danger in jumping to the solution too early is that becoming fixated on functionality will pull the spotlight away from the overlying business goal. In our experience, this is the primary reason most dashboards fail.

> One of the snares of intuitive problem solving is "jumping to design."

At Blue Margin, when setting out to define a dashboard, we start by asking for the goal. Most often, clients point to designs rather than goals, for example, "We need better visibility into orders and inventory." Sounds reasonable. "Understanding orders and inventory" sounds like a goal, but it's actually a design for reaching a goal. There's invariably more to the story. You'll find the rest of the story somewhere underneath the acute symptom of "poor visibility." The real issue is revealed when you thoroughly explore the problem *before* grabbing onto possible solutions.

As a dashboard designer, you'd prefer an answer along the lines of, "We need to decrease our aging inventory to reduce costs." Once the goal is defined, you can more accurately identify what issues are hindering that goal and what insights will mitigate those issues.

Even after you start digging, each unearthed issue will likely re-trigger the impulse to get busy applying fixes. Be careful. Solution design is more about defining the goal (and the issues hindering that goal) than about defining features and functionality. Do the first part right and the second part will virtually reveal itself. Again, if compelling design ideas crop up, you can always put down your shovel, make a note, then get back to digging.

Use the 80/20 filter. The brainstorming process needs to remain fluid. If you become fixated on perfection or try to evaluate the merit of every idea along the way, the process will bog down. You'll find yourself trapped in a binary, pass/fail framework instead of prioritizing issues and simply limiting yourself to the most crucial ones.

So, feel free to write down any and all problems and their causes. Let the ideas flow unhindered. Later, you'll apply a filter to separate the must-haves from the nice-to-haves. Ranking each issue from one to five (five being the most critical), then dismissing the ones and twos (and even the threes) will help you overcome the perfectionism trap. If you struggle to let go of lower-priority issues, console yourself with the idea that once your solution is established, you can go back and address those issues (though in our experience, they'll never qualify as worth fixing).

The process of deciding what's "above-the-line" and what's "below-the-line" is central to developing solutions that stick. Try to fix everything and you'll never arrive at a solution that's simple enough to endure the journey from the whiteboard to the real world.

The 5 BlueCore Steps:

Overview. In its simplest form, the BlueCore process starts with a measurable goal, then lists the successive issues hindering that goal until actionable roots are identified, revealing the simplest, highest-impact solution.

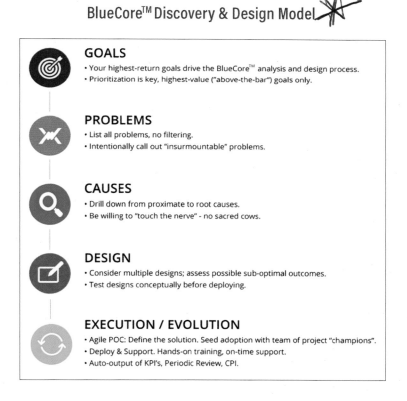

Figure 10. Blue Core Discovery and Design Model.

1. **Define the Goal (in measurable terms)**

   Start by defining what you're after. That may sound easy but will take some effort. Arriving at a well-stated goal that's "at the right level" can be tricky.

   Don't shoot for a goal that's too lofty, nor one that's too tactical. To illustrate, "Improve operational efficiency" is probably too high-level and vague to be useful. On the other hand, "Create a better expense reimbursement form," sounds like a solution in search of a goal.

   A better goal might be, "Decrease our expense-reimbursement time by half." This goal is specific but doesn't dictate a particular design. It also points to a measurable KPI (e.g., "average days to process expense reports"). Defining an empirical measure is central to designing an effective solution.

   If you're having trouble identifying goals for your dashboards, ask yourself the following questions:

   a. What are the company's top three opportunities: what is most exciting about the business currently?

   b. What are the top three business problems the company is currently trying to solve: what keeps executives up at night?

   c. What are the most critical activities, by role, that affect the company's success?

   d. What critical decisions are made on a daily, weekly, and monthly basis that most differentiate the business and make it successful?

   e. How do executives, the management team, and employees currently maintain focus on the right priorities?

2. **List the Problems**

   After a goal has been identified, brainstorm all the problems that hinder the goal. An example problem might be, "Employees don't fill out expense reports correctly." It's a simple statement that doesn't necessarily explain "why" (answering "why" comes next).

After you've listed the problems, rank them 1-5 to determine which are above or below the line.

3. **Identify the Proximate Issues and Root Causes**

    Start with the above-the-line problems and drill down through the proximate issues until you get to root causes. A proximate issue for the above example might be, "The expense form is confusing." Drilling down to the root might take digging deeper. You can get to the root by repeatedly asking *why*. For example, the next level of causation might be that the expense form has redundant fields, or ambiguous wording, or doesn't account for edge-cases.

    By continuing the process, you'll eventually drill down to actionable roots. In our experience, these typically show up three to five layers deep. For example, a root cause might be, "The expense form was designed from a bookkeeper's perspective and doesn't take the end-user's viewpoint into consideration." Or, if you dig even deeper, you may decide the real root is, "There is no system in place for periodically reviewing company forms for ease-of-use and relevance." Either root might be at the right level. You get to decide. Here is where some flexibility and intuition come into play.

    > Rather than applying band-aids, drilling to roots will point to a more foundational solution that doesn't just address the symptoms.

    Take your time getting to the root. In the above example, it might be tempting to take action at the "problem" level by issuing a new policy penalizing employees for incorrectly filling out expense forms (i.e. "Expense forms filled out incorrectly will be returned and will not be eligible for processing until the next cycle."). Rather than applying band-aids, drilling to roots will point to a more foundational solution that doesn't just address the symptoms. For example, "Redesign the expense form to fit the end-user's vocabulary and workflow." By getting to root causes you'll automatically fix all the overlying proximate issues. The result will be more impact and better adoption.

Once you've drilled down to the root cause(s) for a problem, move to the next most important problem and repeat the process. Each problem might have several proximate issues and root causes, which can seem daunting. However, problems often share underlying elements, making the process easier as you go along, similar to how a puzzle becomes progressively simpler with each added piece.

4. **Assess Potential Designs**

You can evaluate the potential efficacy of a design by simply counting how many overlying causes it solves. Additionally, considering possible unintended consequences of each design will help you identify those that introduce the least risk.

However, the most important test for the viability of a design is assessing how efficiently it will advance the KPI(s) defined in the goal. Also, consider how difficult it will be to track those KPIs. Is the performance data a byproduct of normal workflow, or does it have to be separately entered? If the data is already in a transactional system, how accurate is it and how difficult to retrieve? If the cost of acquiring the data outweighs the value of solving the problem, the proposed solution shouldn't make the cut.

5. **Execute and Evolve**

Keep in mind that every design needs room to evolve. Even after carefully following the BlueCore process, your solution will require some iteration before it's running at top-speed. It will also need periodic review to adapt to your evolving business. Keeping KPIs front-and-center will naturally drive that evolution. Also, if you show employees empirically (and visually) how they're performing against goals, you'll harness the strategic problem solver in each, and they'll naturally request adjustments to dashboards as needed.

That said, minimizing course corrections before you launch will greatly increase the likelihood of adoption. End-users will quickly become jaded and will reject new systems if they encounter too many bumps along the way.

BlueCore and Dashboard Development

Since adopting the BlueCore model, we're consistently surprised by the number of otherwise sophisticated businesses that rely heavily on intuition over a structured process to solve problems. Companies often falter at the very first step: defining the goal. Doing so sets a bad trajectory for the rest of the design process, leading to an accumulation of features and functionality that poorly support the goal.

Execution comes down to decisions and actions, so focusing on which decisions and actions are most important is the right place to start when thinking about developing dashboards. It can be tempting to stick with whatever metrics and reports the company has traditionally relied upon. Instead, we recommend setting those legacy reports aside and analyzing exactly how you measure your company's success on a daily basis.

> Companies often falter at the very first step: defining the goal.

Then, simply follow the BlueCore (or other root-cause analysis) model. Ask yourself what most hinders a given goal. For example, if the goal is doubling sales, fearlessly call out every issue that hinders that goal, without regard to how significant the issue is, or how seemingly insurmountable. Don't be afraid to invite the elephants into the room. If the obstacle is daunting (e.g., "We've tried everything we can think of and are out of ideas"), continue brainstorming and you'll be surprised at how many viable solutions present themselves.

Once you've drilled down to a root cause (e.g., "We don't accurately incentivize our salespeople to focus on the right activities"), you can begin designing your dashboard. This is where KPIs do their magic. Keep in mind the axiom that *what gets measured, gets managed.* If you design a solution but have no means of measuring its effectiveness, you'll be back at the same table addressing the same issue before too long.

If you design a solution but have no means of measuring its effectiveness, you'll be back at the same table addressing the same issue before too long.

For KPIs to have value, they must touch a nerve. Creating countless spreadsheets, charts, graphs, and PowerPoints is not the key to changing behavior. The key is to find those few measurements that evoke a response and improve performance. To find them, consider which metrics measure the activities that produce results, rather than measuring the results themselves.

For example, "Closed Sales Per Month in Dollars" is a precise measurement of an outcome, but to change behavior, you should put a spotlight on the activities that *produce* that outcome. Employees won't likely take ownership of KPIs that measure downstream results (such as closed sales) rather than midstream activities.

Figure 11. Blue Margin dashboard with KPIs.

In our experience, KPIs should measure activities that are as close in proximity to the desired result as possible, while remaining largely under the employee's control. "Number of Dials" might seem like a good sales KPI because the employee has near-perfect control over it. However, depending on the business, *dials* might be the farthest point in the sales process from the actual sale, and therefore may be a poor indicator of outcomes.

Additionally, measurements such as *dials*, which are far removed from the desired outcome, are often high in volume and therefore difficult to manage. Validating each dial is impractical, making it easy to game, even if unintentionally. After all, what constitutes a dial? Do misdials or wrong numbers count? How about leaving a message? What about leaving a message at the same number twice in one day? Measuring an

> If KPIs are tied to activities that predict outcomes poorly, employees will have little incentive to hit their numbers.

activity with high subjectivity and frequency creates *noise* that weakens the correlation between the activity and the desired outcome.

If KPIs are tied to activities that predict outcomes poorly, employees will have little incentive to hit their numbers. We learned this lesson from our failed attempt to gamify sales using the rules of baseball. And it's the reason scoreboards in sports include only those metrics that are crucial the goal of winning the game.

You might argue that placing careful parameters on what constitutes a *dial* would solve the problem. However, the more complicated the rules, the higher the likelihood of confusion and poor adoption. Alternatively, you might argue that additional KPIs could be used to motivate employees, but adding too many KPIs can be equally problematic, creating complexities and redundancies that quickly cross the threshold of diminishing returns. For dashboards to take hold, simplicity is essential.

Going to the other extreme, you might decide to measure the number of proposals generated per salesperson, an activity with a high correlation to sales outcomes. The problem with this level of measurement is that the employee may have little control over the results. The likely outcome is that employees will be discouraged rather than motivated by the pressure to perform due to their limited ability to impact the KPI.

Instead of "Proposals Generated," a good KPI might be "Sales Interactions." Each *Interaction* would represent an exchange between the salesperson and a prospective client that advances the sale (one way or the other). "Sales Interactions" is a measure reasonably within an employee's control and it more closely correlates to closed sales than *dials*. Also, measures such as "Sales Interactions" can be reasonably audited. That is, they are fewer in number and have meaningful qualifiers (e.g., With whom? What was discussed?) such that a manager can assess the data behind the KPI.

Ultimately, identifying the right KPIs is often the solution itself. In other words, rather than implementing new systems or processes, simply providing visibility into the right metrics will drive the right outcomes.

> Ultimately, identifying the right KPIs is often the solution itself.

Chapter 11

Design Principles for Dashboard Adoption

Easy and Compelling = Adoption

Through trial and error, we've identified five (and a half) design characteristics that make the difference between dashboards that get ignored
and those that get used consistently over time. These elements will determine
if your reporting is mostly noise or truly compelling and easy enough to take
root.

Figure 12. Five keys to adoption.

1. **Mission Critical.**

   First and foremost, for BI to succeed, it must include only the salient stuff. In other words, if the graph, chart, report, table, or KPI doesn't compel you to pick up the phone, call a meeting, make a decision, shift your focus in some way, or confirm your course, don't include it in the dashboard. Push it to the future (the *waaaay* distant future).

   Otherwise, once your data is organized and in one place, you'll give in to the temptation to believe that *more* is *better*. You'll find yourself thinking, "Since we have the data, let's include it. It might come in handy." There's your red flag. If the best reason you can give for adding a piece of information to a dashboard is, "It might come in handy," or "It's informational," odds are it should be relegated to your sandbox dashboard (the one that scratches an itch, but never gets published). The more you water down your BI environment with nice-to-haves, the less compelling it will be to users, and the less likely they'll come back for more. Ask yourself, "What action will this graph trigger and what decisions will it cause?" If the answers aren't clear, set it aside. With dashboards, less is more.

   Consider the following scoreboard:

Figure 13. Baseball scoreboard. Source: Wikipedia Fair Use.

Even though baseball is a veritable fountain of data and statistics, the above scoreboard displays only the critical information players and fans need to understand exactly what's happening *right now*. Every number on the board touches a nerve and drives decisions and actions in the game.

The Dashboard Effect

2. **Contextual.**

Context brings your data to life. My daughter once asked me to guess how many geese she had seen at the park. I said, "I don't know. How many?" Her answer? "A lot!" To a five-year-old "a lot" could be four, or four hundred. Hard to know without context. Presenting the numbers to your audience might make them feel more informed, but without context, it won't trigger the change in behavior you're seeking.

For example, if you tell your executive committee that the company website received 1.2 million hits last month, it may raise eyebrows, but your audience won't know what to do with the information. If, however, you tell them that the 1.2 million views were an increase of 70 percent over the same period the previous year, and three times the average for companies in the industry, and that sales increased correspondingly, and that the marketing department only spent $1,000 on paid-placement ads prior to the upturn, their response might be, "Why the heck aren't we spending *more* on paid-placement ads??!!"

KPIs provide context. They alert users at a glance to areas of acute opportunity and risk. They spotlight exceptions in the data and tell a story without requiring the user to study the data. Below are two graphs: one with just the numbers, and one with context. Which is more compelling to you?

Limited Context:

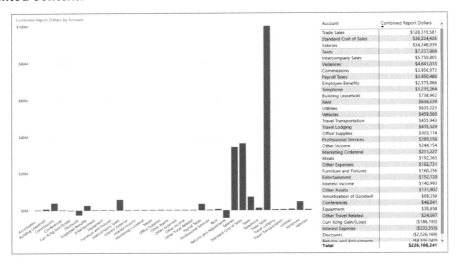

Figure 14. Dashboard without context.

Lots of Context:

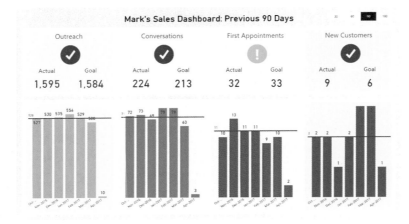

Figure 15. Dashboard with key performance indicators.

The first requires study (and a magnifying glass), and the second instantly calls your attention to a potential issue ("First Appointments").

3. **Highly Accessible.**

Like the dashboard in your car, your data needs to be heads-up and dead simple. If determining your driving speed required logging into an app or doing mental calculations, you'd probably resort to driving by feel and reacting to whatever comes your way. It takes very little friction for people to backslide from being data-driven to being reactionary. If the insights your employees need aren't as easy as grabbing a smart phone and checking the scoreboard, they won't adopt. They're too busy keeping their heads above water add yet more overhead. If you send employees a daily digest of KPIs via e-mail, or display exceptions-based dashboards on TVs around the office, or set the default tabs on their web browsers to the dashboard most relevant to their daily work (or even better, all of the above), you'll begin shifting your culture toward data.

> In our experience, it takes very little friction for people to backslide from being data-driven to being reactionary.

4. **Real Time.**

Keeping your dashboards as current as possible is important for the same reason that yesterday's newspaper is used as fire starter and today's is fought over at the breakfast table (well, it used to be). Why are last year's top-of-the-line golf clubs considered obsolete, though they were hailed as the apex of engineering at the time, and this year's, though virtually indistinguishable, are considered state of the art? People are drawn to what's new. A postmortem view of last month's sales is a chore to digest. By comparison, the success rate of sales interactions this week is exciting. Keep it fresh, and users will consistently come back to check the score.

5. **Graphical.**

Unless you're an accountant who reads numbers like the rest of us read words, graphs are easier to consume than tables. When it comes to data, pictures are truly worth a thousand words (or data points). Although most of our clients already have access to the data they need in table form, once that data is displayed graphically, they invariably respond more viscerally (e.g., "I can't believe we're spending that much time on approving purchase orders!").

A recent University of Illinois study identified the same phenomenon related to nutrition labels. The study discovered that consumers are more likely to make healthy choices when presented with a simple, two-dimensional graph than with a typical nutrition label (i.e., voluminous and undifferentiated "micro-text").[47] Similarly, a Wharton School of Business study found that 67 percent of audience members are persuaded by verbal presentations with accompanying visuals, versus 50 percent by purely verbal presentations.[48]

Maps are a perfect example of why graphical information has more impact than numbers alone. For instance, if you're given a set of tables showing Colorado's production of natural gas by county and asked to determine where the state should consider investing in infrastructure, it might take hours or days to form an opinion. See that same data on a map, and it instantly tells the story.

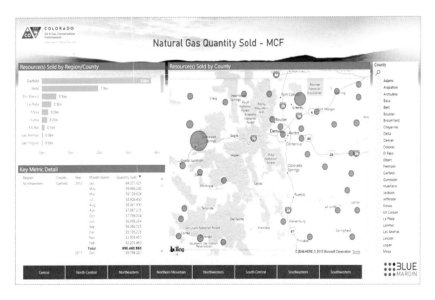

Figure 16. Colorado Oil and Gas Conservation Commission Interactive Map.

Similarly, if you're presented with sales figures for the past six months and asked to forecast sales outcomes going forward, you'd have to hunker down for some analysis. A regression graph, however, delivers instant insight.

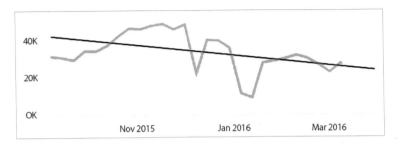

Figure 17. Dashboard conveying sales progress with regression line.

People prefer pictures to raw data the same way they prefer stories over facts. We like stories. Stories stick. And for most of us, pictures tell stories more effectively than numbers.

5.5. Interactive.

For the same reason that smartphones overtook the market, interactive dashboards are more compelling and more likely to get adopted than static reports. Touch-screens, which were revolutionary just a few years ago, are now expected, and the same functionality is quickly becoming the norm for data. Like toddlers in a baby activity center, give us some knobs and noisemakers, and we'll want to keep playing.

By contrast, PowerPoints and PDFs have become synonymous with nap time. If you want your audience to stay awake and keep coming back, give them something to do. A good dashboard, one that gets adopted, should intuitively invite the user to explore the data (and maybe even have some fun).

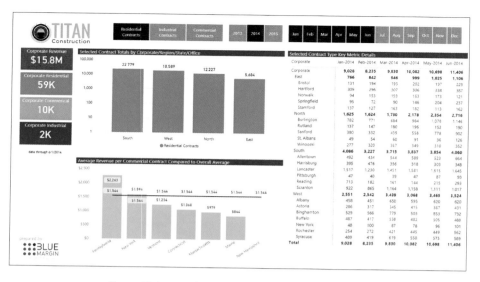

Figure 18. Interactive construction project dashboard.

Figure 19. Future Blue Margin employee.

The Dashboard Effect

Chapter 12

More Keys to Adoption

Even with unprecedented accessibility to data tools, companies often struggle to deploy dashboards that achieve the desired goal. The newest technologies for harnessing and consuming data, though arguably revolutionary, have not created a revolution in data-driven operations for most of the companies we encounter. We're creatures of habit, and habits are hard to break. Intuitively, if you offer a better way to get from point *A* to point *B*, people should naturally jump on board. That's the assumption that leaves so many IT departments scratching their heads. If technology is continually advancing, what causes over 60 percent of IT initiatives to fail?[49]

The cause most often stems from a failure to apply reliable change-management practices to the design and deployment process. Most of us assume that if a new system is an improvement, adoption is a given. After years of deploying data intelligence systems, we've found that's not the case, and we therefore strongly encourage our clients to make change-management a central focus of their BI initiatives.

More than any other factor, for a system to succeed, people need to *use* it. To state the obvious, the world's greatest dashboards won't do any good if people don't look at them. Even mediocre dashboards, if successfully adopted, can make a big difference in your business. Of course, the goal is not mediocre dashboards, but high-impact, actionable dashboards that *get adopted.*

> More than any other factor, for a system to succeed, people need to use it.

In chapter 4 ("But We Already Have Reports Coming out Our Ears!"), we outlined dashboard design elements necessary for engaging end-users and keeping the data-driven side of your business alive and well. Compelling design notwithstanding, well executed change management is also critical to adoption.

The term *change management* can have different meanings depending on your perspective. At its core and in the context of deploying tools for visibility, change management mitigates the gotchas that can (and usually will) derail a BI initiative. Below are eight principals for effectively managing change and further ensuring dashboard adoption.

1. **Dashboards should be goal centric, not feature centric.** When designing new systems, the highest-value business goal should be the start- and end-point, and each aspect of the design should be validated by how well it supports that goal. In other words, the central focus throughout the design process should be the business outcomes, not the features or functionality.

2. **Dashboards should be persona-centric.** A persona (i.e., the end-user's title, responsibilities, success measures, etc.) should be the main character in the story a dashboard tells. Without the persona in mind, you're guaranteed to miss the mark. Ask yourself, "Who is going to consume this dashboard, and what behavior are we trying to encourage or discourage? What decisions and actions are central to this persona's job success?"

3. **Continual process improvement should be an integral component of your BI initiative.** For a system to succeed, it needs to be measured. You'll want to track which dashboards are being used, by whom, and how often. In other words, to affect adoption, you'll want a *dashboard of your dashboards*. This meta-view may be some of the most important data you track. Also, for your dashboards to remain relevant, you should assess their impact on a regular cadence. As your business evolves, dashboards can easily slip into obsolescence.

Sustaining The Dashboard Effect requires a programmatic approach. Resist the temptation to "set it and forget it."

4. **Simpler is better.** To increase the odds of adoption, your BI system should be as simple as possible while still efficiently achieving the goal. Those who deploy new business technologies, whether as employees or consultants, are apt to equate more features and functionality with more value. In our experience the opposite is more often true.

   The overriding change-management principle should not be to design for every use-case, but to overcome the hurdle of adoption. Seek to solve the most acute issues and leave the peripheral issues for later (after adoption has taken hold). After all, without adoption, all your planning and designing, no matter how brilliant, is worthless. As billionaire Richard Branson put it, "Complexity is your enemy. Any fool can make something complicated. It is hard to keep things simple."[50] Once you've established a beachhead, you can (cautiously) add functionality.

   > Uncertainty creates anxiety, but dashboards overcome the conundrum of uncertainty most of us face.

5. **New systems should be tested via proof-of-concept.** The first iterations of your dashboards are best implemented in a POC. The POC can be thought of as a soft launch. That is, before deploying a new system to your full user-base, start with a few select people. The POC serves several purposes. The first is to work out the kinks in the system before broad exposure. Additionally, the POC allows you to build a team of *champions*, those who will get behind the initiative and help seed adoption in the organization.

6. **Your BI initiative should change established processes as little as possible.** Before inventing a better way to do something, be sure to thoroughly understand how users currently accomplish the goal and why they do it that way. You'll find that users aren't consciously aware of why some processes exist, and by digging beneath the surface, you'll

discover business requirements essential to the design.

Understanding the root-cause for established processes will help reveal which elements are needed and which are low-value artifacts or idiosyncrasies. It will enable you to hold onto existing processes wherever possible (assuming they don't hinder the goal) so that users have to change as little as possible. To seed adoption, designs should minimize change while still efficiently meeting the goal.

7. **Successful systems should be formally launched.** A common mistake in deploying new solutions is to downplay the final step—the launch. We assume people will automatically adopt improvements, so it may be tempting to simply inform users via email that new dashboards are available, what the benefits are, and how to use them. This approach may work when users are experiencing significant pain with the incumbent system. Otherwise, resistance to change may outweigh the perceived benefit. A formal launch lends legitimacy to an initiative. It positions the solution as an important and credible change. Moreover, a formal launch is a good justification for switching off old systems so that users aren't tempted to drift back to the familiar.

8. **Training and support are essential.** Combining your formal launch with training and support will reduce the risk that users become confused or frustrated and fail to adopt. We advise training users twice. Sometimes the details from an initial training fail to take hold as trainees struggle to get oriented; they may understand the instructions, but without hands-on familiarity and real-world context, details invariably slip through the cracks. However, after a week working with the system, a second training will help the details stick.

Additionally, once users are trained and using a system, you'll want to provide timely support. Responding quickly enough to keep users from becoming frustrated will ease adoption. If users hit one too many snags, they'll quickly lose excitement for the new, "better" system. Don't give them that opportunity. Make sure they have an easy, picture-book style reference guide to cover the basics and a real human they can talk to when they get stuck.

Chapter 13

Dashboard Deployment (and Worksheet)

After performing a root-case analysis, the solution should be all but self-evident. Operationalizing that solution is the next step. We use the following guidelines to structure the technical and business requirements before building a dashboard. We've added examples for context.

Report Discovery/Definition

Business Requirements
- **Client:** Acme
- **Report Name:** Employee Utilization
- **Report Owner:** Delivery Team
- **Key Resources/SMEs:** Operations Manager
- **Report Goals/Business Outcomes**
  - ▷ Increase employee utilization/productivity by 10 percent; KPIs for hours worked against projects and tickets.
- **Actions/Decisions this Report Drives**
  - ▷ Better understand employee utilization for billable vs. non-billable projects. Forecast demand, capacity, hiring etc.
- **Report Users/Audience:** Executive team, and individual operators
- **Delivery Cadence:** Ad-hoc Power BI Report
- **Data Update Cadence:** Auto-refresh daily

- **Delivery Methods:** Publish to Power BI workspace, daily email digest, office monitors
- **RLS or Other Security Requirements**
    ▷ Role-based security model setup to the individual
    ▷ Individuals will see their numbers, top-level team, and organization numbers. Individuals will only see summarized data.
- **Business Process Supported:** Employee utilization and productivity
- **Existing Report:** There are some default ERP Reports and mash-ups in Excel
- **New Report/Dashboard Description:** (Visuals, tables, cards, etc.) Top cards: Utilization % with KPI, Capacity % with KPI, Stacked column chart—break-out of total hours (billable, OOF, etc.) per month/week. Bullet chart of utilization vs. Goal.
- **Slicers:** Year, Month, Department, Supervisor, Employee, Project
- **Drill-downs:** None
- **Drill-through Sub-reports:** Individual employee utilization details
- **Aesthetic requirements:** Client logo and color theme from website
- **Acceptance Criteria:** Reporting data to be validated to source. Data Quality Services to address anomalies.
- **Exclusions:** N/A

Questions to Vet a Proposed Dashboard Design:

It may seem repetitive, but once a dashboard has been designed, it pays to do a final vetting before turning it over to end-users. The goal isn't to produce a *perfect* dashboard, but to make any reasonable improvements that maximize the odds of adoption.

1. Are any elements "just informational?" That's a red flag. Each should drive specific decisions/actions.
2. What performance areas will be improved?
    a. What is the status of KPIs and measures currently (even if subjective – e.g., "Our sales productivity is currently at a C+")?

      b. What is the goal for those measures and KPIs?

  3. What is the story? What should the user's internal narrative be when viewing the dashboard?

      a. E.g., "I'm the business owner. I want to optimize utilization..."

Additional Guidelines for Successful Dashboard Design:

1. The greatest value of a dashboard is simply bringing data together in a way that is easy to consume. In other words, don't over-engineer. Keep it simple; only critical information should make the cut.

2. Shifting time from the build phase to the planning phase almost always produces better results, faster.

3. Consistent page structure dramatically improves ease-of-use and adoption (e.g., consistent refresh date and slicer locations, similar types of information in the same quadrants across reports, etc.).

4. Don't start building a report until after you've created a wireframe/storyboard and solicited feedback from stakeholders.

5. Keep report titles simple and intuitive.

6. Place slicers (filters) on the right-hand side of the page; try to answer users' most immediate questions at the top of the slicer stack.

7. Put the company logo in the upper-left corner of the page.

8. Include a "data freshness" date under the company logo.

9. Shoot for a maximum of 3-4 visuals per report. There are four types of information that make up a majority of reports we develop: current state; trend; context (or KPI), and detail (typically a table showing transaction-level data).

10. KPI's should be prominent in the design. They provide strong visual clues for performance (e.g., green checkmarks, red X's).

11. Don't use KPI colors in other visuals. For example, if green is used for good and red for bad, don't use them in a bar chart unless those meanings apply. Colors should be used with a purpose. Arbitrary coloring may look nice but will add complexity.

The Dashboard Effect

12. Minimize digits on the screen. For example, if $1.9M does the trick, don't show it as $1,912,543, or if 24% conveys the meaning needed, don't show it as 24.32%.

13. Text should be consistent in terms of font, size, and color. For visualization titles, use a larger font.

14. Use snap-to-grid functionality, if available. Everything should line up and be distributed in a balanced and consistent way.

15. Consider report backgrounds carefully. Bias toward white or "clean" backgrounds.

The Dashboard Effect

SECTION FOUR

The Tools of Visibility

Chapter 14

A New Breed of Business Intelligence

The Dashboard Effect, at its core uses data to drive productivity and growth. It takes an honest view of the good news and the bad, embraces hard truths, and accommodates a culture of open feedback. It provides access to information throughout the company and uses empirical data to highlight issues and opportunities early.

Never before has data been so available to nontechnical business users, and never before have there been so many low-cost, turnkey services for operationalizing transparency. The up-and-coming leaders in business are those who recognize this sea-change and embrace growing revolution in data. Those who hold fast to outmoded conventions will continue to fight against the current.

If you haven't investigated business intelligence technologies lately, you'll likely be shocked by the number of affordable and

> Never before have there been so many low-cost, turnkey services for operationalizing transparency.

user-friendly platforms on the market. Many (if not most) are offered via SaaS (i.e., Software as a Service, or Cloud-based software) because SaaS offers several advantages over on-premises solutions, including:

- Faster deployment
- Lower technical hurdles
- Lower total cost of ownership
- Automated backup and disaster recovery

- Access from virtually anywhere, any device
- Ease of use ((i.e., user-interface more frequently updated to current standards)
- Elastic scalability
- Enterprise-class security

The field of available SaaS BI platforms is diverse, with niche tools that address a growing number of use-cases. The more complete solutions can do everything from automatically gathering and shaping data to calculating measures, creating visuals, and disseminating reports to employees, partners, and customers. Each has its strengths and weaknesses, though several are clear market leaders, including Tableau, Qlik, and Power BI, to name a few. Reviewing the features and functionality of even a subset of available BI platforms doesn't fit the scope of this book, and because Cloud-based tools evolve rapidly, any technical description would merely be a snapshot in time.

That said, we'll profile one of the leading systems, Microsoft's Power BI, because it represents a comprehensive solution and therefore is a good example of the breadth of functionality available in mainstream BI tools. Also, it's what we know best. Objectively, Power BI ranks as a leader in the category (according to prominent industry benchmarks, including those by Gartner and Forrester). Subjectively, and by way of disclosure, Blue Margin is a Microsoft Partner. Nonetheless, our business is best served by specializing in whatever platform has the broadest market appeal. We've hitched our wagon to Power BI because it's the most viable solution in most of the cases we encounter. That could change, and since we're not employees of Microsoft, we would switch platforms accordingly. For now, we're firmly in the Microsoft camp.

While acknowledging that when you're a hammer the world looks like a nail, we'll do our best offer an objective view of Power BI's more noteworthy features.

Power BI

Power BI is the brand name of Microsoft's stand-alone, SaaS BI platform. It grew out of Excel's BI toolset and shares many of Excel's fundamental components. Surprisingly, most Excel users aren't aware their go-to spreadsheet contains a robust set of BI tools, including PowerPivot (for data-modeling), PowerQuery (for extracting data from transactional systems, transforming it, and loading it into a data model), PowerView (for creating visuals), and DAX (or Data Analysis Expressions, for building and applying functions that generate measures, KPI's, and calculated columns).

Why would Microsoft create two sets of similar BI tools, one built in Excel and the other in Power BI, a separate, stand-alone service? There are several possible motives. The most likely is a function of development velocity. Because Excel is the most ubiquitous data tool on the planet (with over one billion instances deployed), any updates risk introducing a bug, or bugs, on a massive scale. That risk is why updates to major platforms like Excel require meticulous change management and therefore lengthy release cycles.

Power BI, by contrast, is built-for-purpose to create and share visual analytics. Because of its narrower scope, its release cycle is much shorter than Excel's, allowing Microsoft to add functionality at a fast clip (typically monthly).

While having two toolsets might seem confusing, the upside is versatility. No matter your use-cases for business intelligence, Excel will likely continue to play a role in your business (at least until you pry it from your financial analysts' cold, dead hands). Therefore, being aware that Excel offers data modeling and analysis tools will serve you well.

For now, we'll focus on Power BI, Excel's more nimble business-intelligence sibling.

Key Differentiators

Many leading BI solutions offer similar functionality to Power BI, including:

- **ETL (Extract, Transform, Load)**. This allows users to connect to data sources (e.g., accounting software), extract data on an automated schedule, transform that data (e.g., convert number formats, perform search-and-replace, delete duplicates), and load it into a reporting data model.

- **Data Modeling**. This function replaces the need to use Excel's "VLOOKUPs" and other arduous tools for relating data across tables. Most data modeling tools also include a graphic interface called an ERD (entity relationship diagram) that allows users to drag and drop tables and create relationships visually.
- **Measures and Calculated Columns**. To create measures, most BI tools offer the ability to apply functions to the data. This is useful for aggregating and analyzing data. For example, rather than separately tracking refunds and replacements, you might also want to track the ratio between them. Time-slicing and statistical analysis also require the use of functions.
- **Charts and Graphs**. Of course, the end-goal of any BI tool is to make data impactful and easy to consume. Nothing does this better than visual analytics. Most BI tools offer several visualization templates and enable you to combine and cross-filter visuals with tabular data (i.e., tables) on the same dashboard, creating a more complete picture.

Beyond these common tools, Power BI has some key differentiators, including:

- Exceptionally low cost (in some cases, an order of magnitude lower than leading competitors)
- Rapid (monthly) development release cycle
- Tight Excel integration and familiar functionality for Excel users
- Open-source visualizations (there are currently over one-hundred community-developed visual templates available on Microsoft's appsource.com, in addition to Power BI's out-of-the-box templates)

These distinctions have made Power BI a true market disruptor.

If you're skeptical that an enterprise like Microsoft, which missed the boat on other key trends (e.g., Windows Phone), can take the form of a well-funded tech start-up and disrupt an established market, we don't blame you.

> What's the likelihood a corporation that develops thousands of products in hundreds of categories could successfully take on industry-leading, built-for-purpose platforms like Tableau and Qlik? Not good.

Microsoft has long been trying to shake their reputation as a de-facto monopoly that subsists on Windows' entrenched position as the default operating system for most of the world's computers. After all, what's the likelihood a corporation that develops thousands of products in hundreds of product categories could successfully take on industry-leading, built-for-purpose platforms like Tableau and Qlik? Not good.

But Microsoft capitalized on several unique advantages, not the least of which was a change of leadership. With the departure of Steve Balmer, the image of being an out-of-touch, closed-door organization (and the painful YouTube reminders of "Monkeyboy" and other blunders) finally came to an end. The entrance of Satya Nadella did much to overcome the stereotype of the fat-cat CEO who couldn't get in step with the times. Microsoft's new CEO began opening doors that had long been closed, reaching out to rivals like Apple, Salesforce, and Box.com to form strategic alliances. He brought that same approach to Power BI, opening the source-code for its visual templates to the developer community and incentivizing the development of new and innovative ways of viewing data.

Additionally, Microsoft leveraged its "second-comer advantage." Watching industry leaders like Tableau spend over a decade establishing the market demand for self-serve BI, Microsoft dug into its deep well of intellectual property around data and analytics (primarily Excel and SQL Server) to develop a competitive solution. Since these assets had already paid for themselves,

Microsoft had a distinct advantage in terms of development costs. In contrast to competitors like Domo (which notoriously raised over $450 million in investment capital), Microsoft had already monetized the data tools it would use as the building blocks of Power BI.[51] As a result, Microsoft has been able to price its offering well below its competition.

Microsoft also has the ability to put all the resources of a massive enterprise behind an in-house startup. Launched in July of 2015, more than twelve years after Tableau's launch, Power BI pulled into the lead in the category (per Gartner and Forrester) in under twelve months.[52] It achieved its frontrunner status by doing something nearly unprecedented in the world of enterprise software development. That is, from the point of launching the service (when Power BI was not, in our opinion, *ready for prime time*) until and beyond the point when it became a category leader, the Power BI team delivered on a breakneck development cycle, releasing a new set of features every month. The result has been a continuous flood of new functionality. By departing from their traditional waterfall development model where big feature-updates are delivered infrequently, Microsoft achieved success in penetrating an established, fast-evolving market.

Lastly, Microsoft has the unique advantage of owning many of the productivity and analysis platforms companies use every day, tools which integrate well with Power BI. Examples include SQL Server, SharePoint, and Microsoft Office (most notably, Excel).

With its home-team advantage, it's not surprising that Power BI plays well with Excel. Excel tables and charts can be published onto the Power BI "canvas" with ease, and Excel can connect to Power BI, essentially *borrowing* its data model. This means you can pick up in Excel where you left off in Power BI, rather than exporting raw data into Excel and starting from scratch. And you can automatically update spreadsheets connected to Power BI as the data is refreshed. Similarly, a PowerPivot data model built in Excel can be imported directly into Power BI.

Rob Collie, author of several books on Microsoft's data platform, put it this way: "New capabilities in PowerPivot 'rhyme with' the things you already know in Excel" (see all of Rob's technical insights and hilarious musings at powerpivotpro.com).[53] PowerPivot

is the same data modeling tool found in both Excel and Power BI, meaning those familiar with Excel (i.e., most professionals with a computer) can pick up Power BI skills quickly.

Chapter 15

The Data Warehouse

Ultimately, the quality of your dashboards will be limited to the quality of your data. Therefore, you'll need a way to gather, organize, and clean your data to make it dashboard-ready. Data can be difficult to wrangle, and most companies are overwhelmed by the complexity and chaos of their data ecosystem. Data can quickly spin out of control even in a simple business, and getting it corralled can seem like an insurmountable task.

Your company probably generates data from numerous sources, including systems for accounting, sales, operations, marketing, and HR, to name a few. The number of sources may shock you. Even small start-ups can have ten or more data sources. Though designed to help improve efficiency, software systems can also sabotage progress by creating silos of information.

When information is siloed across an organization, manually generating a cohesive view of performance can prove nearly impossible. Leaving your data disconnected will hinder your ability to compete in a market where companies are increasingly leveraging data to their advantage. For data to be useful, it must be gathered, distilled, and connected.

Raw data pulled straight from transactional systems is generally not reporting-friendly, but that can be overcome. Think of your data as a jigsaw puzzle. Each piece is virtually meaningless on its own. Gathering all the pieces into a pile doesn't improve the situation much. But start organizing them by type and fitting them together, and patterns emerge to eventually reveal the big picture. This is the role of the data warehouse.

Excel Data Management: Square Peg, Round Hole

However, the tool most commonly used in business to gather and organize data is *not* the data warehouse. It's Excel. While virtually indispensable, Excel files are rarely governed and can therefore easily proliferate, having the ironic effect of exacerbating a company's data entropy.

How many of these Excel headaches ring true at your company?

- High-cost resources spend countless hours assembling and manipulating Excel reports instead of engaging in their highest and best use.
- Someone uses an outdated version of an Excel file, resulting in wasted work.
- Two people make changes to a shared Excel file at the same time, causing one to be overwritten.
- An Excel file with critical data, perhaps the only copy, is lost in the chaos of e-mails, shared-drives, and folders.
- A shared spreadsheet is deleted by someone who doesn't realize it's still needed by others.
- Someone changes a workbook, inadvertently breaking macros, linked workbooks, and reports.
- An Excel file can't be accessed because it lives on the laptop of someone who is out sick, or at an appointment, or trekking through the remote jungles of NoDataServiceHere.

Trying to tame your business data through a melee of Excel files is decidedly frustrating. We've seen it over and over. Excel-dependent organizations are perpetually hampered by missing, faulty, and/or outdated data.

The Right Tool for the Job

While importing your Excel data into a single dashboarding tool (such as Tableau or Power BI) may cut back the Excel jungle to a degree, it won't create the foundation needed for a scalable, data-driven business. Mashing-up your data in this way is a poor solution because BI tools aren't specifically designed to organize and process data; they don't have the robustness and scalability most companies need to get control of their data.

So how do you build a business intelligence system that's robust and scalable enough to evolve with your business? You guessed it—with a data warehouse.

A data warehouse is the single, structured repository where all your data is organized so it can be put to good use. It's the sole source of truth for your company and is foundational to The Dashboard Effect.

Building a data warehouse can seem ominous. If you don't have a data architect on staff, you may worry that data warehouses are the exclusive domain of other, uber-technical companies. Ten years ago, you would have been right, but today virtually any business can join the data revolution. Data warehouses are many times easier and more affordable to deploy than just a few years ago.

Nonetheless, for most of us the value of a data warehouse can seem purely academic or obscured by *instead-of* reasoning: "You should build a data warehouse *instead of* _____" (instead of using Excel, instead of connecting your data directly to a BI tool, instead of generating reports directly from your operational systems). Even for those reasons, there's a cost and complexity threshold where migrating to a data warehouse makes obvious sense. Up until that point, however, a data warehouse may seem like an unnecessary expense.

Until you consider *technical debt*.

Technical debt is the recurring expense that results from taking shortcuts now. Without a data warehouse, you're left mashing up your data from several sources into a single file. In this mash-up scenario, the painful cost comes when you want to add or change data sources or change reporting platforms. Heck, even updating a source system to its latest version can break your reporting (which can be costly to fix).

If your business uses a BI tool to mash up your data, then your data architecture will look a lot like this:

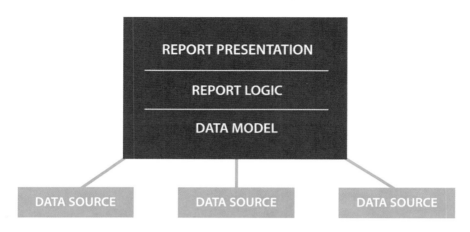

Reporting platform with report model built by mashing up
data sources inside of the platform

Figure 20. High-level view of typical data mash-up.

In academic terms this means your data model inevitably ends up encapsulating your report logic, and that in turn is encapsulated by the reporting platform, tightly binding the report logic to the report presentation layer.

In nonacademic terms this means that if you ever want to change one part of the system, you end up having to change all the parts (remember those old TV-VCR mash-up units? Same issue). Also, if you change a field or column in your CRM or accounting system, your mash-up tool will simply return a system error. Moreover, if you ever want to migrate to a new reporting platform, chances are you'll be able to reuse little of your work.

But if you use a data warehouse, your architecture will no longer look like the above classic *bad example* and will instead have a much better structure (note the Denver Broncos colors):

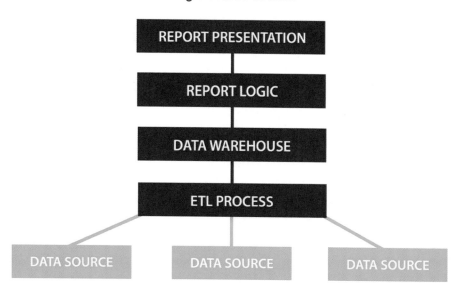

Reporting platform using a data warehouse as the single source of data

| REPORT PRESENTATION |
| REPORT LOGIC |
| DATA WAREHOUSE |
| ETL PROCESS |

DATA SOURCE   DATA SOURCE   DATA SOURCE

Figure 21. Data warehouse designed for flexibility and scalability.

With a Data Warehouse, no single tier of your architecture is tightly bound to another. You can change your ETL, save money by switching your business software, or switch your reporting platform to the latest and greatest. Whatever the change, you only need to worry about that one component rather than the entire stack. And if you add or delete a column from your CRM or accounting tool, your reports will still work rather than returning a general error (though they will need updating if you want to include the changed data).

Here's another important benefit of data warehouses that often gets overlooked. What happens when you want to use multiple reporting tools? With mash-up tools, you'll have to recreate the data model in each, assuming those reporting tools even have ETL and data-modeling functionality. With a data warehouse, you can simply connect those reporting tools to the system.

Reporting using a robust data warehouse with connected platforms

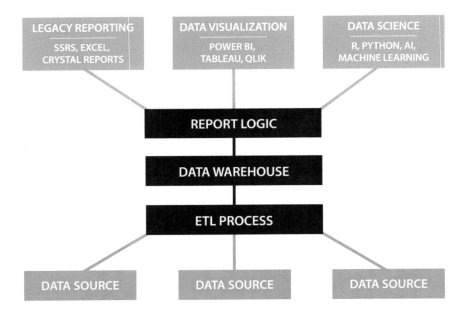

Figure 22. Robust data warehouse with connected reporting platforms.

Other considerations:

- A data warehouse protects your business systems.
    - ▷ By minimizing direct access to your transactional software, you avoid impacting the performance of those systems and the risk that someone will mishandle them.
- A data warehouse is the single source of truth.
    - ▷ Unlike Excel, there's no risk you're using the wrong version of your data because everyone is accessing the same central source.
    - ▷ Also, a properly designed data warehouse is "aware" of how current its data is, so users can know how up-to-date the information is.
- A data warehouse is ACID.
    - ▷ In computer science ACID (Atomicity, Consistency, Isolation,

Durability) is a set of properties that ensures database transactions are processed reliably.

- A data warehouse maintains historical accuracy and historical context.
  - ▷ Consider this scenario: You have two teams of salespeople. Your sales report shows total sales by team, by week. One team is significantly outperforming the other, so you decide to mix up the players to even out the teams. When you look at your report for the previous week, it *should* reflect the sales figures for the teams as they were configured at that time.

    A system that doesn't maintain historical context will instead suggest that the teams were performing evenly the previous week, because the system is only aware of its current state and responds as though the *current* team assignments have *always* been the team assignments.

- A data warehouse can hold massive quantities of data.
  - ▷ Excel holds smaller quantities, less efficiently. Various BI tools may hold data, but accessing that data is often limited (some Cloud API's will even throttle your data transfer after a certain amount of usage, making them poor choices for real-time reporting).

- A data warehouse is fast.
  - ▷ Desktop reporting tools are limited to the power of the desktop. The typical business computer may not be up to the task. A data warehouse on multicore servers with gobs of RAM and a speedy disk array is much more powerful; let it do the heavy lifting.
  - ▷ Speed is important and here's why. If an employee has to wait sixty seconds for a report to run and has to run that report five times daily over the course of a year, he or she will spend more than twenty hours waiting. For an employee making $75,000/year, that's over $750 in wages spent *just waiting*.

Not to mention the fact that the employee may stop using the report altogether out of frustration.

- Data warehouses can be made regulation compliant (e.g., SOX, PCI, FERPA, HIPAA, SSAE16).
  - ▷ Cloud-based BI services have variable compliance profiles, requiring you to work around limitations. Excel files on their own are *never* standards-compliant; additional controls must be placed around the access to and distribution of those files.
  - ▷ A data warehouse enables you to have a single compliance profile for a single, master repository of your data.
- A data warehouse is secure.
  - ▷ You can control access through user-credentials and manage exactly who can access what.
  - ▷ You can enforce who is allowed to modify data and who can only view data.
  - ▷ You can easily audit every aspect of a data warehouse—who has access to what, what data was modified when, what the value of the data was before it was modified, etc.
- A data warehouse is reliable.
  - ▷ You can capture your data at any level of granularity.
  - ▷ In the event of a disaster, you can restore your data to a specific point in time.
  - ▷ You can set up a redundant infrastructure (e.g., server clustering, regional instances, etc.).
- Data warehouses are affordable.
  - ▷ Cloud-based servers that can be rented for as little as $100 per month typically provide more storage and processing power than many companies need.
  - ▷ There are FOSS (free and open-source software) options.
    - ▪ Database engines like PostGRE, MySQL, MongoDB, and MariaDB.

- SQL Server Express is free, and it includes a good subset of SSRS functionality (an enterprise-class reporting tool).
- A data warehouse lets you *own your data* (and avoid being held hostage by your software providers).
  - ▷ What happens to your reports when your provider changes how their data connectors work?
  - ▷ What happens to your data when your provider increases rates to a level you're unwilling to pay?
  - ▷ When a data provider serves up *all* your data, how do you control what can be seen by specific groups of users (e.g., sales managers, financial analysts, senior executives, etc.)?
- Beating the drum here—choosing not to build a data warehouse is taking on technical debt. It's a debt that demands payment, yet never gets paid down. And it's fraught with gotchas.
  - ▷ Want to change the Cloud service provider for one of your key applications? With a data warehouse, you only need to update your ETL to bring the new source in to your existing structure. By contrast, if you use a data mashup tool, you'll also need to update your data model and likely the reports it feeds.
  - ▷ Want to change your reporting tool? You'll need to rebuild your entire data model. Data warehouses are designed with reporting in mind, regardless of which reporting tool you use.
  - ▷ Need to tackle big data? Data mashup tools don't offer the performance you need.
  - ▷ Plan on scaling up? As your number of data sources grows, the ETL and data model in your mash-up system will become unwieldy and unstable.

Chapter 16

The How of Data Warehousing

Deploying a data warehouse requires some technical expertise, causing many businesses to push their data strategy to the back burner. They assume it will be too expensive and won't provide a quick return on investment.

A short time ago, that reasoning might have been sound. Even now, purchasing and setting up the servers and software licenses needed for an in-house data warehouse *is* expensive and complex. Maintaining it requires a combination of several areas of expertise. And the licensing can be steep, pushing your ROI beyond the horizon.

Enter the Cloud.

Cloud-based business intelligence systems are an appealing option for virtually every business, enabling not only enterprises to cut costs, but bringing enterprise-grade BI within the reach of small and midsized businesses. Cloud-based offerings by companies like Amazon, Microsoft, Google, and Rackspace provide services ranging from virtual server "stacks" to narrower, specific services such as single hosted database instances and web applications.

So how does the Cloud help you put your data to work? We've already discussed the *why* of storing your data in a centralized location (i.e., ownership, ease-of-use, scalability, security, etc.). Now let's discuss the *how*—specifically in the Cloud.

Virtually everything you can do with computing on-premises you can now do in the Cloud. One of the main benefits of the Cloud is that you don't have to buy the hardware, maintain it, and replace it when it gets old. And you

---

don't have to create a data center (or the dreaded *data closet*), simplifying your company's IT infrastructure. Also, with Cloud services, you won't have to create your own security infrastructure, remote connectivity, or redundancy (not all Cloud infrastructure services automatically include redundancy and backup, but they typically make it an easy add-on).

SaaS for data management enables companies to own a subscription to virtual database tools, rather than leasing or owning a comprehensive infrastructure. A typical subscription includes server licenses, hardware, data-center infrastructure, and the ability to add software modules and support services. Equally important, you can spin resources up or down as needed. Try saving money by turning off your company's in-house data center at the end of each day (hint: it won't be easy, you won't save much, and your IT department will probably go on strike), and you'll understand the benefit of on-demand services.

Bottom line—the Cloud drastically reduces the buy-in cost of standing up a data warehouse. It evens the playing field for non-enterprises, making data analytics and dashboards accessible to many businesses for the first time and lowering the overhead of data management for companies at all levels. What used to cost six figures can now be had for a reasonable monthly fee, replacing big capital costs with much smaller operational costs.

> Bottom line, the Cloud drastically reduces the buy-in cost of standing up a data warehouse. It evens the playing field for non-enterprises, making data analytics and dashboards accessible to many businesses for the first time and lowering the overhead of data management for companies at all levels.

Despite the tremendous advantages of the Cloud, it's not magic. Data won't organize itself. To get control of your data, you'll need someone who understands data architecture. If you have the appetite and time, you can learn most of what you need to know from the web and from books. Of course, there's no substitute for experience, and unless you were born with the "data gene" (unscientifically estimated by Rob Collie to be one in fifteen people), you may need the help of an expert. That said, even with an expert on board, you'll want a basic working knowledge, so you can ensure your own success.

If you want to gain a deeper understanding of data warehousing, we recommend starting with *The Data Warehouse Toolkit*, third edition, by Ralph Kimball.[54]

Chapter 17

A Data Management Primer

D ata management is a science unto itself, with unique nomenclature, systems, and best practices. Below are some common terms you'll run into as you work with your data. You don't need technical mastery of the following, but a basic knowledge will help you stay in the conversation.

OLTP versus OLAP

- **OLTP**, or Online Transaction Processing, writes data quickly and reliably to and from transactional software systems, such as Great Plains, Salesforce, Dynamics, etc. The structure isn't optimal for reporting, as data is often stored in granular bits and pieces that need to be reconstituted to form the whole, rather than larger *chunks* of data ripe for analysis. OLTP is not meant for analysis; that's the job of the data warehouse. Moreover, connecting your reporting tool directly to an OLTP system can negatively impact the system's performance.
- **OLAP**, or Online Analytics Processing, is a system for storing data specifically for analytical processing. You'll hear folks referring to *OLAP Cubes*. It may sound super "sciencey," but don't be intimidated. It simply refers to a method of organizing data so that it's optimized for reporting. It will often include pre-summarized measures (e.g., Net Profit) sliced by various dimensions (e.g., by store, by month), making it much easier and faster for the average businessperson to query the data for the information they need. OLAP cubes are structured to deal

with large amounts of data and return results quickly. This is most likely the data model you'll use to feed your reports and dashboards.

Data Modeling

Data models consist of related tables of data. Data tables contain the raw material needed to populate your reports and dashboards. Below are the two most common types of tables and how they relate.

Fact Table. Fact tables contain the output data from transactions or events. For example, a construction company will capture transaction data for a project, including hours worked and dollars spent on labor and materials. This data is typically numerical and therefore suitable for calculating measures (e.g., total cost).

Dimension Table. Dimensions describe, filter, and/or group the facts. In other words, they apply *dimension* or *perspective* to your facts. An example of a dimension might be a list of your clients (whereas facts might include the number and cost of items sold to those clients). Generally, anything in a fact table can be aggregated, whereas anything in a dimension table is what you use to aggregate those facts.

Relating Facts and Dimensions

Tables can be related in various schemas, depending on your objective (or your preference). The two most common schemas are *star* and *snowflake*. Do a search and you'll find a hotly contested debate over which is better for reporting data models (in most cases, we favor the star schema, per Ralph Kimball). To get started you only need to know what they are.

In a star schema, fact tables are connected directly to dimensions. Simple as that. This model is centered around facts and therefore is good for producing metrics, such as the total revenue for a given customer and/or given time period.

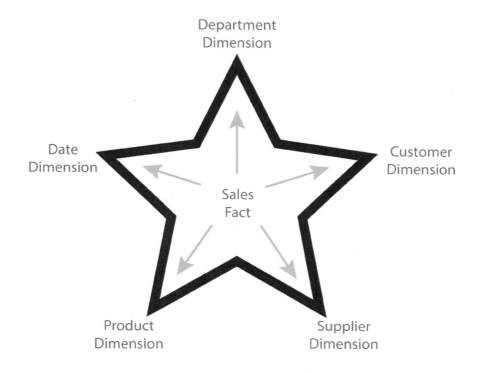

Figure 23. Star schema to organize data for reporting.

In a snowflake schema, the data is organized to minimize redundancy and keep data volume to a minimum. Rather than connecting only to facts, dimensions can have their own dimensions. A snowflake schema is better for some types of analysis. However, it has a higher number of joins between tables, which can potentially slow performance and make writing measures more complex.

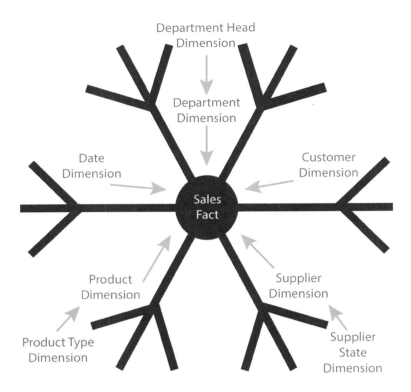

Figure 24. Snowflake schema.

Entity Relationship Diagram, or ERD

Like the OLAP Cube, this one sounds impressive, but it's simply the term for a diagram that illustrates the relationships between fact and dimension tables in a database (like the star and snowflake examples above). Here's an example:

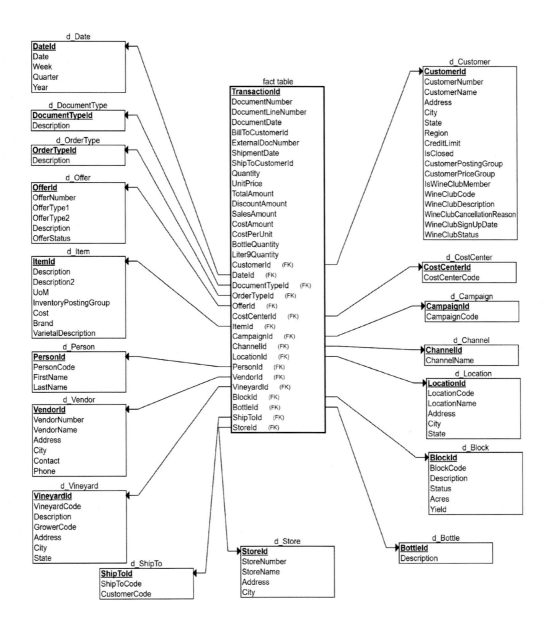

Figure 25. Entity Relationship Diagram.

Data Marts and How They Differ from Data Warehouses

Unlike the all-encompassing data warehouse, data marts typically have a specific focus (e.g., sales, finance, production, warranty). They are also simpler to build, including only a slice of the overall data. Depending on your goals and data environment (or your data expert's preferred best-practice), your strategy may call for building either the warehouse or the marts first. Some experts would argue that the warehouse should come first and that marts should be developed as a by-product. Others prefer to build marts first, then assemble the warehouse by aggregating the marts.

Operational Data Store, or ODS

An ODS is simply a copy of one or more transactional databases. It stops short of offering report-ready dimensions and measures. For some businesses, an ODS is as far as they care to take their data-management strategy, and frankly it's better than nothing. It may lack the power of a reporting cube, but it's simple to create, removes reporting overhead from transactional systems, and provides a basic foundation for reporting.

ETL

Storing data is the easy part, at least compared to the process of transforming and moving data. When you're looking to move your data from its source to a data warehouse, you're going to need an ETL tool. ETL stands for Extract, Transform, and Load. Examples of ETL tools include Informatica, SQL Server Integration Services (SSIS), Scribe, and Azure Data Factory. These tools take data from one or more sources, modify that data in some manner (e.g., converting times to a local time zone, euros to dollars, transactions to totals), and deliver it to the appropriate destination.

In other words, ETL tools enable you to *extract* data from a source, *transform* it to make it more report-ready, and *load* it into your data warehouse. For your data initiative to succeed, your ETL processes must be efficient and accurate. Your business can't pause while your data loads, and you can't afford for your data to be untrustworthy. If you base critical decisions on your data, it must paint a reliable, timely picture.

Yet ETL processes are susceptible to breaking when data sources change. Ironically, when that happens, it's time to pop the champagne and celebrate, because that's the goal! The ETL broke, *not* the reports. To fix the issue, all you need to do is fix the broken ETL component(s); the rest of your data warehouse and data-visualization platform won't be affected. That distinction can be the difference between twenty hours of work and two hundred.

SECTION FIVE

The Big Picture

Chapter 18

The Dashboard Effect and Your Success

Data is changing the way we do business. It has the power to elevate accountability and initiative. It can increase motivation and create a sense of ownership at all levels of an organization. It helps keep everyone focused on common, measurable goals, and it removes the barriers between managers and employees. However, change is difficult to initiate. If your business is operating reactively and if you have no time to develop tools for visibility, know that by starting small (i.e., one problem, one data source, and one dashboard), you can lay the foundation for The Dashboard Effect and make positive changes to your organization in a matter of weeks, not months.

By adapting the principles of this book to your unique business and by embracing transparency and implementing dashboards, you'll quickly develop your own brand of The Dashboard Effect. We've experienced the dramatic impact it brings and have helped many other companies do the same. Our goal is not simply to deploy dashboards. That's a design, not a goal. The goal is organizational transformation—to create an honest, transparent view of your business that brings out the best in you and your employees.

For Blue Margin, the greatest benefit of The Dashboard Effect is empowering our employees. As executives, we know how easy it is to become a slave to our business. We're also acutely aware that entrepreneurs who know how to bring a business to life often don't know how to hand it off (or at least parts of it) to others. This can be a significant limiter to scaling any business. Rather than job satisfaction, businesses are often as likely to deliver seventy-hour workweeks and burnout to those at the wheel. But by giving employees greater visibility, you're giving them the keys to the car. Allow them to take the wheel, and free yourself to focus on your highest and best use.

What could you do if your employees had the same level of visibility and sense of responsibility as you? What's your highest and best use to the company, and are you able to spend time on those activities? A culture of visibility will free you and your organization to achieve more by empowering those around you.

> For Blue Margin, the greatest benefit of The Dashboard Effect is empowering our employees.

With data's barrier-to-entry at its lowest point ever, don't wait to start transforming your organization. Even a small start can have you experiencing The Dashboard Effect in short order.

Visibility Beyond Business

The Dashboard Effect is about being transparent, not just with the company's performance but with one another. While the utilitarian goal of a business is profit, that's not the whole story. A business is made up of people, and reducing their value to mere financial contribution misses an opportunity for true, long-term success. Being transparent means recognizing that businesses affect people, whether employees, clients, or the broader community. Those who embrace the full potential of their business, who focus on the value they bring to others, will add depth and meaning to their effort, melding their work life with the rest of life and creating an enduring organizations people want to be part of.

So please allow us a brief digression into the most important ingredient of *our* Dashboard Effect.

If your life's work is to make enough money for retirement, or if the centerpiece of your legacy is wealth, research says you'll be disappointed when you reach the end. All the toil, the risk and worry, and the deprioritization of relationships can't be overcome with money. Regardless of your worldview, research indicates that your greatest satisfaction and significance comes from connecting with and impacting others. In a *US News and World Report* article titled "Why Relationships Are Crucial to Your Health and Happiness," world-renowned psychologist Chris Peterson sums up his decades of research with the simple axiom that "other people matter." His overriding conclusion is that our connections to other people may be the greatest determiner of our well-being *and* our material success.[55]

At Blue Margin, understanding what most matters came into focus several years ago as we approached a new year and decided to reexamine our vision for the company. There were the usual business goals around growth, profitability, culture, and market positioning. But somehow the turning of another year made us more contemplative, more aware of the big *whys*. Growth and profitability are good things, but to what end? The obvious answer, "Because it brings value to our clients and feeds our families in the process," didn't fully close the loop.

Maybe it wasn't the new year. Maybe it was our increasingly graying hair. Regardless, our profitability goals began taking a back seat to our *impact* goals. Eventually we arrived at an epiphany—it's too easy to find comfort in the word *someday*. *Someday I'll have more time; someday I'll have more money; someday I'll have more energy...someday I'll (fill in the blank)*. The problem is that *someday*, by definition, never comes.

> It's too easy to find comfort in the word "someday."

We wondered if we could start impacting people *now*, rather than waiting until we (someday) created surplus wealth. We decided to begin by elevating volunteerism in our company. We initially envisioned monthlong well-digging trips to Africa, but with the limited resources of a startup, we developed a plan to start small and serve locally. With this idea in mind, we've implemented a community works program (cleverly named "Blue Margin Community Works"). The program pays employees to volunteer each month. It also rewards employees who complete certain levels of community service by donating to the charity of their choice for each milestone reached.

The Dashboard Effect

According to a survey by the US Office of Research and Policy Development, volunteering reduces illness, lowers stress, and increases happiness.[56] And those are just the benefits to the volunteer, let alone those receiving help. Nonetheless, as perennial entrepreneurs, we've had to fight our instinct to always keep our foot on the gas. We're taking the words of Winston Churchill on faith: "We make a living by what we do, but we make a life by what we give."[57]

We're not trying to preach. We still have a lot to learn, and we want you to be as profitable as possible, because if your business stagnates, your ability to impact others will also stagnate. The Dashboard Effect is predicated on the fact that job descriptions and micromanagement are no longer the best ways to draw out employees' potential. Engaging the whole person, giving employees the visibility they need to take ownership of their work, and empowering them to impact others—that's the surest path to growth, stability, and lasting success.

It would be difficult to communicate the sense of well-being and common purpose that fills our office when we return from reading books to underprivileged kids or serving food at a homeless shelter. There may be no single factor that contributes more to the health of our company and culture. And yes, we have a dashboard for our volunteer hours.

We understand our perspective is just that—*our* perspective. We've participated in many businesses, and each is unique. So, we offer our story without the illusion that we have found *the way*, knowing full well that we continue to wrestle with our shortcomings every day. Rather, we're offering one illustration of how transparency can transform a company and the lives it touches. We hope that in it you find the inspiration to change your own story for the better, and that you'll share your story with us.

Feel free to visit us online at www.bluemargin.com, and encourage us with your Dashboard Effect journey.

The Dashboard Effect

Endnotes

[1] Patel 2015

[2] Singh 2013

[3] Chamorro-Premuzic 2013

[4] Rock and Jones 2015

[5] Coonradt and Nelson 2012

[6] *IBID*, 16

[7] *IBID*, 40

[8] *IBID*, 53-54

[9] *IBID*, xi

[10] Whittick 2015

[11] *IBID*

[12] Morgan 2015

[13] Denning 2015

[14] Morgan 2015

[15] United States Department of Labor 2016

[16] James 2013

[17] Chamorro-Premuzic and Garrad 2017

[18] Lee and Lebowitz 2015

[19] Vance 2015

[20] Lai 2012

[21] Constantine 2016

[22] Beal 2014

[23] Afshar 2014

[24] Davenport 2012

[25] Glassdoor 2017

[26] McGill 2015

[27] Sareen n.d.

[28] Stetler 2014

[29] Bersin 2014

[30] Crabtree 2013

[31] Bersin 2014

[32] Patel 2014

[33] Regalado 2013

[34] Manjoo 2015

[35] Ferro 2016

[36] National Transportation Safety Board Office of Public Affairs 2000

[37] Small Business Administration: Office of Advocacy 2011

[38] Consumer Reports 2014

[39] Belmont 2011

[40] Badkar 2014

[41] Harter 2015

[42] Glassdoor for Employers 2015

[43] Bureau 2017

[44] Egham 2015

[45] ASQ 2006

[46] ASQ 2009

[47] University of Illinois: College of Agricultural, Consumer and Environmental Sciences 2016

[48] Ashton 2015

[49] Krigsman 2008

[50] Andersen 2013

[51] Hesseldahl 2015

[52] Sallam, et al. 2017

[53] Collie 2013

[54] Kimble and Ross 2013

[55] Davis-Laack 2014

[56] Sareen n.d.

[57] Kiprilov 2015

Bibliography

Afshar, Vala. 2014. "50 Stunning Mobile Facts And Statistics." *Huffington Post*. February 12. Accessed April 14, 2017. http://www.huffingtonpost.com/vala-afshar/50-stunning-mobile-facts_b_4440213.html.

Andersen, Erika. 2013. "11 Quotes from Sir Richard Branson on Business, Leadership, and Passion." *Forbes*. March 16. Accessed April 17, 2017. https://www.forbes.com/sites/erikaandersen/2013/03/16/11-quotes-from-sir-richard-branson-on-business-leadership-and-passion/#292e3f-1b69e7.

Ashton, Danny. 2015. "10 Reasons Why You Should Care About Visual Content Marketing." *NeoMam Studios*. February 19. Accessed April 14, 2017. http://neomam.com/blog/13reasons.

ASQ. 2009. *The Define Measure Analyze Improve Control (DMAIC) Process*. Accessed April 18, 2017. http://asq.org/learn-about-quality/six-sigma/overview/dmaic.html.

—. 2006. *What is Root Cause Analysis (RCA)?* Accessed April 18, 2017. http://asq.org/learn-about-quality/root-cause-analysis/overview/overview.html.

Badkar, Mamta. 2014. *The 16 Biggest Corporate Mega-Deals Of All Time*. February 13. Accessed April 14, 2017. http://www.businessinsider.com/16-biggest-acquisitions-of-all-time-2014-2.

Beal, Vangie. 2014. "15 Important Big Data Facts for IT Professionals." *Webopedia*. February 4. Accessed April 2017, 2017. http://www.webopedia.com/quick_ref/important-big-data-facts-for-it-professionals.html.

Belmont, David. 2011. *Managing Hedge Fund Risk and Financing: Adapting to a New Era*. Singapore: John Wiley & Sons.

Bersin, Josh. 2014. "Thrive: How to Build a Simply Irresistible™ Organization." *LinkedIn*. March 27. Accessed April 14, 2017. https://www.linkedin.com/pulse/20140327162423-131079-thrive-how-to-build-a-simply-irresistible-organization.

Bureau, Gadgets Now. 2018. *Gadgets Now*. May 24. Accessed August 1, 2018. https://www.gadgetsnow.com/slideshows/10-highest-selling-smartphones-revealed/apple-iphone-6s/photolist/57859682.cms.

Chamorro-Premuzic, Thomas. 2013. "Motivating People: Does Money Really Affect Motivation? A Review of the Research." *Harvard Business Review*. April 10. Accessed April 13, 2017. https://hbr.org/2013/04/does-money-really-affect-motiv.

Chamorro-Premuzic, Thomas, and Lewis Garrad. 2017. "If You Want to Motivate Employees, Stop Trusting Your Instincts." *Harvard Business Review*. February 8. Accessed April 13, 2017. https://hbr.org/2017/02/if-you-want-to-motivate-employees-stop-trusting-your-instincts?utm_campaign=hbr&utm_source=fa.

Collie, Rob. 2013. *DAX Formulas for PowerPivot*. Meritt Island: Holy Macro! Books.

Constantine, Josh. 2016. "Slack's growth is insane, with daily user count up 3.5X in a year." *TechCrunch*. April 1. Accessed April 13, 2017. https://techcrunch.com/2016/04/01/rocketship-emoji/.

Consumer Reports. 2014. "How to find a great car mechanic." *Consumer Reports*. October. Accessed April 14, 2017. http://www.consumerreports.org/cro/2012/12/how-to-find-a-great-car-mechanic/index.htm.

Coonradt, Charles A., and Lee Nelson. 2012. *The Game of Work*. Layton: Gibbs Smith.

Crabtree, Steve. 2013. "Worldwide, 13% of Employees Are Engaged at Work." *Gallup.* October 8. Accessed April 14, 2017. http://www.gallup.com/poll/165269/worldwide-employees-engaged-work.aspx.

Davenport, Thomas H. and Patil, D.J. 2012. "Data Scientist: The Sexiest Job of the 21st Century." *Harvard Business Review.* October. Accessed October 3, 2017. https://hbr.org/2012/10/data-scientist-the-sexiest-job-of-the-21st-century.

Davis-Laack, Paula. 2014. "Why Relationships are Crucial to Your Health and Happiness." *U.S. News and World Report.* October 9. Accessed April 18, 2017. http://health.usnews.com/health-news/blogs/eat-run/2014/10/09/why-relationships-are-crucial-to-your-health-and-happiness.

Denning, Steve. 2015. "Is Holacracy Succeeding At Zappos?" *Forbes.* May 23. Accessed April 13, 2017. www.forbes.com/sites/stevedenning/2015/05/23/is-holacracy-succeeding-at-zappos/.

Egham. 2015. *Gartner.* September 15. Accessed November 1, 2017. https://www.gartner.com/newsroom/id/3130017.

Ferro, Shane. 2016. "What Happened When This Major Company Got Rid Of All Its Bosses." *Huffington Post.* January 26. Accessed April 14, 2017. http://www.huffingtonpost.com/entry/why-you-need-a-boss_us_569fddd-be4b0fca5ba765409.

Glassdoor. 2017. "50 Best Jobs in America." *Glassdoor.* Accessed October 3, 2017. https://www.glassdoor.com/List/Best-Jobs-in-America-LST_KQ0,20.htm.

Glassdoor for Employers. 2015. *Top HR Statistics.* Accessed April 2017. https://www.glassdoor.com/employers/popular-topics/hr-stats.htm.

Harter, Jim. 2015. "Gallup." *Obsolete Annual Reviews.* September 28. Accessed April 14, 2017. http://www.gallup.com/opinion/gallup/185921/obsolete-annual-reviews-gallup-advice.aspx?utm_source=alert&utm_medium=email&utm_content=morelink&utm_campaign=syndication.

Hesseldahl, Arik. 2015. *BlackRock Leads $200 Million Round in Domo at $2 Billion Valuation.* April 8. Accessed July 3, 2017. https://www.recode.net/2015/4/8/11561232/blackrock-leads-200-million-round-in-domo-at-2-billion-valuation.

James, Geoffrey. 2013. "10 Things Employees Want More Than a Raise." *Inc. com.* October 7. Accessed April 13, 2017. http://www.inc.com/geoffrey-james/10-things-employees-want-more-than-a-raise.html.

Kimble, Ralph, and Margy Ross. 2013. *The data warehouse toolkit : the definitive guide to dimensional modeling.* Indianapolis: Wiley.

Kiprilov, Nicole. 2015. *Discovering a Journey Through Writing.* Amazon Digital Services, LLC.

Krigsman, Michael. 2008. "Study: 68 percent of IT projects fail." *ZDNet.* December 11. http://www.zdnet.com/article/study-68-percent-of-it-projects-fail-6103001175/.

Lai, Eric. 2012. "Average Mobile Worker Carries 3.5 Devices. Here's the Downside." *ZDNet.* May 11. Accessed April 13, 2017. http://www.zdnet.com/article/average-mobile-worker-carries-3-5-devices-heres-the-downside/.

Lee, Samantha , and Shana Lebowitz. 2015. "20 cognitive biases that screw up your decisions." *Business Insider.* August 26. Accessed April 13, 2017. http://www.businessinsider.com/cognitive-biases-that-affect-decisions-2015-8.

Manjoo, Farhad. 2015. "Slack, the Office Messaging App That May Finally Sink Email." *The New York Times.* March 11. Accessed May 19, 2017. https://www.nytimes.com/2015/03/12/technology/slack-the-office-messaging-app-that-may-finally-sink-email.html?_r=0.

McGill, Justin. 2015. "Why these 9 companies choose transparency." *The Next Web.* March 28. Accessed April 14, 2015. https://thenextweb.com/entrepreneur/2015/03/28/why-these-9-companies-choose-transparency/#.tnw_UKubkMsv.

Morgan, Jacob. 2015. "Behind The Scenes Of The World's Most Transparent Company." *Forbes*. February 19. Accessed April 13, 2017. www.forbes.com/sites/jacobmorgan/2015/02/19/behind-the-scenes-of-the-worlds-most-transparent-company/#b7fb59055c4f.

National Transportation Safety Board Office of Public Affairs. 2000. *NTSB releases final report on investigation of crash of aircraft piloted by John F. Kennedy Jr.* Washington D.C., July 6.

Patel, Neil. 2015. "90% Of Startups Fail: Here's What You Need To Know About The 10%." *Forbes*. January 16. Accessed August 3, 2017. https://www.forbes.com/sites/neilpatel/2015/01/16/90-of-startups-will-fail-heres-what-you-need-to-know-about-the-10/#7755f3d36679.

—. 2014. "Why a Transparent Culture is Good for Business." *Fast Company*. October 9. Accessed April 14, 2017. https://www.fastcompany.com/3036794/why-a-transparent-culture-is-good-for-business.

Regalado, Antonio. 2013. "The Data Made Me Do It: The next frontier for big data is the individual." *MIT Technology Review*. May 3. Accessed April 14, 2017. https://www.technologyreview.com/s/514346/the-data-made-me-do-it/ .

Rock, David, and Beth Jones. 2015. *Harvard Business Review*. September 8. Accessed April 3, 2018. https://hbr.org/2015/09/why-more-and-more-companies-are-ditching-performance-ratings.

Sallam, Rita L., Cindi Howson, Thomas W. Oestreich, James Laurence Richardson, and Joao Tapadinhas. 2017. *Magic Quadrant for Business Intelligence and Analytics Platforms*. Research, Stamford: Gartner .

Sareen, Himanshu. n.d. "An Economy of Trust: How Transparency Is Changing the Tech Industry." *Wired*. Accessed April 14, 2017. https://www.wired.com/insights/2015/03/economy-trust-transparency-changing-tech-industry/.

Singh, Gurjeet. 2013. *The Big Data World is Operating at 1 Percent*. March 10. Accessed August 3, 2017. https://gigaom.com/2013/03/10/the-big-data-world-is-operating-at-1-percent/.

Small Business Administration: Office of Advocacy. 2011. "FAQ: Advocacy: the voice of small business in government." *Small Business Administration.* January. Accessed April 14, 2017. https://www.sba.gov/sites/default/files/sbfaq.pdf.

Stetler, Michael. 2014. "How Transparency Can Affect Employee Productivity." *Advanced Business Coaching.* October 20. Accessed April 14, 2017. http://www.abcbizcoach.com/business-coaching-consulting/how-transparency-can-affect-employee-productivity/.

United States Department of Labor. 2016. *Economic News Release: Employee Tenure in 2016.* Washington D.C.: Bureau of Labor Statistics.

University of Illinois: College of Agricultural, Consumer and Environmental Sciences. 2016. "Graphical display of nutrition information helps keep health-conscious eaters on target." *ScienceDaily.* February 4. Accessed April 6, 2017. https://www.sciencedaily.com/releases/2016/02/160204175632.htm.

Vance, Jeff. 2015. "Datamation." *Big Data Analytics Overview.* June 8. Accessed April 14, 2017. www.datamation.com/applications/big-data-analytics-overview.html.

Whittick, Simon. 2015. *Research Report: One in Four Employees Leave Due to Mushroom Management.* September 21. Accessed April 13, 2017. www.geckoboard.com/blog/research-report-one-in-four-employees-leave-due-to-mushroom-management/#.VzTat_krKUk.

Acknowledgements

This book … several years in the making, has many contributors and many people to thank. First, to Ed Daniels, our partner and long-time friend, thank you for helping us on this publishing journey. Thanks also to Kevin McManus and Chris Piekarz for your insights and contributions. Sara Sanders—you are the Zen master. Jim Harrington—our first client—thanks for having faith in us. Sadie Henry, for getting us through the "basement years." Thanks also to Beth Florin for encouraging us to write this book, and to Andy Thompson for holding our feet to the fire. To our early advisors, Chris Christopher, David Cunningham, and all the great folks at Rocky Mountain Innosphere, we needed your guidance to make the Blue Margin journey a reality. Thank you also to Richard Cook, Stacy Slinkard, and Richard Fagerlin for your proofs and input. To Tracy Mueller, thank you for forging a road less travelled and inspiring us in countless ways. To Mitch Majeski, Mike Handley, David Diehl, and Mike McCurdie, thank you for generously sharing your business experience. And to our counterparts around the country, Rob Collie, Scott Senkeresty, and Derek Rickard, here's to a bright future!

To Monique and Stacey for encouraging us every step of the way. "Thank you" will never say enough. And to the entire Thompson family, your support has been unwavering, and we are grateful.

To the entire staff at Blue Margin, we thank you for contributing to every idea in this book. We wouldn't want to be on this journey without you:

Angela Tourney	Joshua Klenk
Kyle Williams	Sebastien Dutot
Courtney Tewalt	Sarah Martinez
Adithya Nanduri	Madeleine Ellender
Lauren Dittmann	Hunter Creech
Paul Van Ryn	Marty St. John
Caleb Ochs	Derek Lusk
Landon Ochs	Jake Burns
Matt Dunn	

About Blue Margin, Inc.

Founded in 2011, Blue Margin, Inc. believes that progress depends on clear visibility into performance, understanding what's working, what's not, and what influences those outcomes. Our exclusive mission is to help other companies capitalize on the benefits of The Dashboard Effect™, where performance metrics remain top-of-mind, empowers everyone from the CEO down to make the right decisions and focus on the right priorities, in real-time.

Authors

Jon Thompson has over 20 years of start-up and executive experience. His emphasis has been in emerging business technologies. In 2000, he and his brother (Brick Thompson) founded Vercuity, a SaaS company that grew into the largest telecom cost-control company in the US, raising over $80M in venture funding and private equity and expanding to over 500 employees. Jon is a student of the data-driven business model and is a recognized writer and speaker on the topic.

Brick Thompson has been a technology "wonk" since birth and has deep roots in data analytics and Cloud computing. He has founded three successful companies, was CEO of Vercuity (backed by One Equity Partners), and EVP of Operations and Software Development at RMD Networks,

backed by Sevin Rosen Funds. Brick also consulted as a program manager in the trading-IT department of the world's largest hedge fund. His broad experience makes him particularly adept at bridging the gap between business operations and technology.